Golden Girls

Golden Girls

Advice and Inspiration for
Today's Grandmothers

SALLY FELDMAN

T

Troubador Publishing Ltd
Unit E2 Airfield Business Park
Harrison Road, Market Harborough
Leicestershire LE16 7UL
Tel: 0116 279 2299
Email: books@troubador.co.uk
Web: www.troubador.co.uk

ISBN 978 1 83628 014 9

British Library Cataloguing in Publication Data.
A catalogue record for this book is available from the British Library.

Printed and bound in Great Britain by 4edge Limited
Typeset in 11pt Minion Pro by Troubador Publishing Ltd, Leicester, UK

Contents

Acknowledgements

I'd like to thank all of the doughty, funny, wise and generous grandmothers who have shared their stories with me – especially my five supergrans, Anna Coote, Maggie Fordham, Linda Hall, Carolyn Meggitt and Tess Woodcraft.

And thank you, Emilia Grace Hall, whose arrival inspired this book.

Introduction

Congratulations to all new grandmothers! You're joining a huge, varied, international and deliciously life-affirming club, and this book is a celebration of all of you.

I've chosen to concentrate on grannies, rather than grandparents in general, because there is truly something exceptional about you. It's now recognised that across the world grandmothers play a crucial role for families, not just helping out with the children, but in some countries even contributing to their survival.

A recent study found that you may be more connected to your grandchildren than to your own children. You are likely to feel greater emotional empathy for the younger generation. "If their grandchild is smiling, they're feeling the child's joy," it concludes. "And if their grandchild is crying, they're feeling the child's pain and distress." So the relationship between you and your grandchildren is uniquely special.

When I became a grandmother I wondered how I might approach this precious new status. Considering a variety of possible role models, including a few celebrity homages to their own grandmas, I set out to discover the art of becoming a granny. This book is the result.

Armed with a lorryload of advice and a plethora of stories, I'll take you on a journey through the first magical years, beginning with the news of a pregnancy: the excitement, the sheer pleasure, but also the anxiety: concern for the expectant mother and the baby. How do grandmothers adjust to their new identity, or to the fear of suddenly being seen as old?

There are more practical matters to consider, too. What will your grandchild call you? How will parents choose to announce the sex of the baby? How will you feel about the name they have chosen?

How much should you tell the expectant mother about the birth? What are the experiences of grandmothers who are there for the big moment? This is so often a moment of bonding and joy. But what if it goes wrong? Here is advice on how to support the parents over miscarriage or stillbirth, as well as what your role should be if a child is born with a disability or with special needs.

If your daughter is a single parent she'll be far more likely to rely on you for help during those early months. But how will you feel if she has gone it alone by resorting to a sperm bank?

Then what happens when the baby finally arrives and you are truly a grandmother? Do you rush round with champagne, balloons and babygros? Or might you be disappointed when the parents keep you away because they just want to be alone? You want to be there to offer support, but when does helping become interfering? Although it's tempting to offer advice, are you aware how much has changed since the time you had your children?

Some of the advice running through this book can be difficult for new grannies to follow. I recommend two principles: listen; and seal your lips. Let the parents tell you about their rules and values, and try not to transgress them. But sometimes you will find yourself bursting to contradict them. For example, how should you respond if they decide not to have the baby inoculated?

Babies are often welcomed with christenings or the sort of secular naming ceremonies that I conduct as a celebrant. So here are some examples of these delightfully warm and happy gatherings, where grandmothers are very often given a central role. I also offer some ideas for presents for the newborn.

After the first sleep-tortured weeks many parents will realise they need you for babysitting, so you'll need to brush up on your nappy-changing expertise, as well as techniques for easing aching teeth or soothing endless screaming.

Almost two in ten of the nation's grandparents provide regular childcare for their children's children. That's around five million grandparents. How should you make your house child-safe? What activities work best? How do you strike a balance between helping and being exploited? While most parents are grateful for your support, there are bound to be conflicts. So what are the best ways to resolve them?

Many grandmothers think it's natural to spoil the children: it's their right. But what's the truth behind spoiling? Sigmund Freud observed that children and grandparents are allied against their shared enemy – the parents. Although it's seen by grannies as a gesture of love, spoiling can be an act of hostility, too.

So what strategies do the parents devise to encourage you to curb these excesses? And how should you respond? After all, the arrival of a new member of the family will entail new adjustments, and new dilemmas. Conflicts can arise, for example, if the two sets of grandparents compete for the affection of the child, often by trying to outdo each other with increasingly extravagant presents. Many grannies find it painful to realise that their adored son loves someone more than them – which can lead to rivalry between granny and daughter-in-law.

Next, to a sacred grandmother hallmark: food, the ultimate gift of love. The eyes of grown people will frequently mist over as they remember the tastes of their childhood: Bubbe's unbeatable chicken soup, or the whole family gathering round the table for a proper Sunday lunch at Nana's house. For families who have been uprooted or dispersed, grandmother's food brings a special comfort, representing the continuity of cultural traditions and identities.

There was a time, not long ago, when newly married couples would move in with his or her parents. Those arrangements often caused friction. But over the past century family dynamics have changed considerably, most dramatically with the radical housing reforms instigated after the Second World War. Slum clearance meant tight-knit family networks were broken up as young couples moved out into the new estates. Since then, more couples have been able to set up their own homes, or have had to travel far across the country – or even further. Many grannies have told me about the difficulties and sometimes the heartbreak of being far from their grandchildren. How do long-distance grannies maintain contact with the children? This can be so painful after a divorce, especially when grandparents are drawn into marital battles.

Lately, families are beginning to share homes once again. With the rocketing price of housing, young couples are increasingly having to depend on their parents' hospitality. Recently arrived immigrant families also tend to live in multi-generational houses. So how do different families adapt to having a live-in granny? How does the relationship change when you're all under the same roof?

Grandmothers have traditionally been portrayed in popular culture as frail, lonely and hobbling. But over the past few years a new heroine has emerged: the bad granny. Here you can meet the wise, angry, wicked and funny grandmothers on the big and small screen, in literature and in children's books.

Finally, the real-life rebels: grandmothers across the world who are working together to make it a better place. That is a legacy so many of us share. What values. principles and wisdom do grandmothers wish to pass on? We end with a homage to grannies everywhere and how very vital they are.

If you're about to become a grandmother for the first time, I hope this book will support you through any of the challenges you may face, and be a companion as you enter this happy chapter in your life.

One

"We Are a Grandmother"

We were tucking into *spaghetti vongole* in a favourite restaurant when my daughter Scarlett told me and her father that she was pregnant. My heart jolted, tears sprang unbidden to my eyes, and for once in my life I was speechless. I could only mutter, "So that explains why you're not drinking."

Slowly the news and its implications became clearer. I was going to be a grandmother. What did that mean? What did grandmothers do? Would I be up to the task? What difference would it make to my own life?

Becoming a grandmother is a rite of passage: much like getting your first period, or losing your virginity. So many of the grandmothers I spoke to felt unprepared for their new role. Along with the excitement came new anxieties: the pregnancy; the birth; would the baby be okay?

They began to look at themselves differently, too. For some, being a grandmother was a symbol of ageing, of being "past it", of becoming the invisible older woman: an unwelcome reminder of mortality. "I hate the idea of being an old lady, but even worse, an ancient grandmother," Bobby told me. "It's so difficult knowing that I won't be around to see them grow up."

You don't choose to be a grandmother, and not everyone loves the idea. Some people just feel they're too young to take on such a role, or they simply don't see it as part of their identity. For others the biggest shock is the recognition that their own baby is now taking on their role as a parent. "It took a while to adjust to the idea of my little boy as a father," remembered Linda. "It wasn't that long ago that he was in nappies himself. Now he'd be changing them. And then I started wondering whether, at 71, I'd be fit enough to be a granny. My own mother was just 39!"

"Get fit," my friend Tess advised when she heard the news. "Go into training now. A little weight-lifting so you can carry the baby without going into back spasms, and something aerobic, to keep up with all the crawling and toddling."

Sheila Hancock sees her grandchildren as a compensation for growing old. "There's a feeling of continuation," she said. "I know that when I go, which will be shortly, there will be people going on who have in them a tiny bit of me."

Even the ultra-glamorous Joanna Lumley has started to think about changing her image. "I'm going to be a little bit more of a granny," she announced a few years ago, "which involves eating a lot of cake and becoming quite big. I want to have one of those housecoat overalls, a nice big one so I get a bit Demis Roussos about it …"

"I've just heard I'm going to be a grandmother," the comedienne Jenny Éclair wrote to *Waitrose* magazine. "In an odd way, I feel the same sense of bewilderment and joy that

I did when I first became a mother... I want to be a good nana, but I'm not sure what this entails. I think in future it means putting protective sheeting over the good sofa, blockading the stairs and trying not to mind when they bring a truckload of plastic toys with them – what's wrong with a simple wooden spinning top? I also think I need to buy a bun-baking tray and start acclimatising to watching cartoons without reaching for the headache pills."

I felt much the same way at first. So I decided to do something that would definitely make me feel like a granny. I started knitting. So did Linda, my daughter's mother-in-law. This experiment was fairly short-lived. My one jumper and one tiny cardigan were a disaster; I even had to send them to Linda to sew together, but they still looked like woolly rags. Meanwhile, she was turning out beautiful little blankets and pram sets.

So I abandoned the enterprise, and, as I threw out the knitting needles, I also resolved to discard the tired old stereotypes regularly touted by the media: that we're either frail, ancient, hobbling, lonely old biddies, or the equally cliched antithesis, "battling grannies" or "granny heroines". The very word "granny" has become a shorthand for "old lady": a handy way to define us by our age and dwindling status.

It's still glibly assumed that once a woman becomes a grandmother everything else in her life is irrelevant. That's absurdly out of date. The average age a woman becomes a grandmother is 47: a far cry from retirement age and leaving plenty of time for her to continue working or realising her ambitions. MP Angela Rayner, who, in her early 40s, is the youngest grandmother in Parliament, doesn't appear to see any conflict between the two roles.

Even so, when Hillary Clinton was running for US President in 2016 she was lampooned as Grandmother-in-Chief, prompting doubts about her suitability for the White House. "Describing a professional woman as a 'grandmother' isn't only reducing her to her familial role, but also implies a hint of shock at the idea of older women's capability," raged Laura Bates, author of *Everyday Sexism*.

So if you, like me, would like to adopt a more positive style, which role will you choose? You might like the idea of being a wise, all-seeing elder: someone who knows the names of flowers, and which herbs will soothe an aching head or calm a scabbed knee. Someone who will always be ready with helpful homilies, a fund of stories and exhaustive knowledge of family history. Everyone will feel safe with the wise granny, turn to her for advice and believe that somehow she knows everything about everything. Most of all, the wise granny will be a natural teacher.

"I am where I am today because my grandmother gave me the foundation for success," said Oprah Winfrey, who lived with her grandmother Hattie Mae Lee on a farm in Mississippi until she was six years old. Oprah learned to read by the age of three, memorised Bible verses and often spoke at her grandmother's church. She credits her with instilling in her the value of education and even helping to develop her public speaking skills.

If you don't feel quite wise enough to take on such a daunting persona, perhaps you'd be happier with becoming a Glam Gran, as defined by Jane Fearnley-Whittingstall in *The Good Granny Guide*.

"She descends on the newborn's cradle like a fairy godmother bearing gifts of designer baby clothes, cashmere wraps and Tiffany teething rings. The Glam Gran won't ever be the nappy-changing, nose-wiping type. Being warm-hearted, she is always keen to take the baby in her arms for a cuddle, but as soon as she detects damp at either end, she passes the parcel. She doesn't really do babies, darling. But she will come into her own when her grandchildren are older, helping them paint their toenails with her nail varnish, giving brilliant presents and thinking up wonderful treats."

That's a lot to live up to. It might be better to stick with what you know. If, like me, you are passionate about women's rights, for example, you could become Feminist Granny: waging a war against gender-specific toys, explaining to toddlers the evils of the patriarchy, taking them on demonstrations and teaching them politically charged nursery rhymes like this:

What are little girls made of
What are little girls made of
Sun and rain and heart and brain
That's what little girls are made of
What are little boys made of
What are little boys made of
Except for little things much the same
That's what little boys are made of.

But if you find that too twee and, frankly, a bit preachy, why not introduce the children instead to the great songs of your own youth? Teach them to harmonise to "Bye, Bye Love", to clap along with "Yellow Submarine" and to love Elvis, Dylan and Joni Mitchell. Then you could qualify as a rock'n'roll granny like Elton John's "lovely nan" Ivy Sewell. It was on her piano that he first discovered his amazing musical talent, and he adored her. In her later years she moved in with him and stayed until she died in 1995.

When she collected her Album Of The Year at the 2024 Brits, the singer Raye called her grandmother Agatha Dawson to the stage. "I want to thank my grandma for her prayers. My grandma is awake until three a.m. praying for me and my beautiful sisters. I love you so much."

Singer-songwriter Katy Perry is another musical star who loves her grandmother, Ann Hudson. She often brings her to awards shows and premieres – the Grammy Award, the Billboard Music Awards – and once even to meet President Obama. At the *Smurfs 2* premiere, Ann walked the red carpet with Perry, wearing a shirt that said, "I've got the hots for Papa Smurf."

That irrepressible attitude is tempting. But maybe you'd rather be more powerful. In which case you could become a matriarch, the head of a dynasty, someone who would command respect – maybe even fear. Though perhaps not quite as terrifying as Lady Olenna Tyrell in *Game of Thrones*, who has a habit of killing her enemies.

A gentler version is the most famous matriarch of them all: the late Queen.

"I think I speak for my generation when I say that the example and continuity provided by The Queen is not only very rare among leaders but a great source of pride and reassurance," said her grandson Prince William. "Time and again, quietly and modestly, The Queen has shown us all that we can confidently embrace the future without compromising the things that are important.

"I am privileged to witness the private side of The Queen, as a grandmother and great-grandmother. The Queen's kindness and sense of humour, her innate sense of calm and perspective, and her love of family and home were all attributes I experienced first-hand."

Despite these admirable qualities the Queen was no pushover. "As I learned from growing up," he admitted, "you don't mess with your grandmother."

I'd certainly like to be a wise and gentle grandmother, especially one that you don't mess with. But I'd also like to emulate strong women who defy the old assumptions about what is expected of them. In other words, my aim is to become Supergran.

But I soon realised it was time to stop thinking about myself, and instead to concentrate on how best to support the expectant mother. A woman whose daughter is pregnant may worry about how much to tell her about the experience of labour. You don't want to terrify her, but neither should you gloss over the realities. Broadcaster and journalist Jenni Murray, who had her second child on the kitchen floor, said it was just like shelling peas. But it's certainly not like that for many of us, and if the account is too breezy the expectant mother could be in for a nasty shock when the time comes.

So maybe it's better to say nothing at all. But it can be enormously comforting for women to hear their mothers' own memories of labour, however dramatic. Whether you gave birth in a taxi or were rushed into surgery, endured 48 gruelling hours or got high on pethidine, at least you are still very much here.

Most expectant parents will have had some form of ante-natal preparation, so you may be expected to share all that, too. I don't remember gleaning much wisdom when we attended the hospital's ante-natal course before my first child was born in the early '80s. We all had to stuff pillows under our jumpers with partners holding our heads while they learned how to help with breathing. Dads asked pertinent questions like "If she eats garlic will it go into the milk?"

Nowadays eager parents will join one of the courses run by the National Childbirth Trust, and will often be lulled into a quiet confidence. As one grandmother advised in *Saga* magazine: "Try not to laugh when the expectant couple come back from their latest ante-natal class and tell you how beautiful natural childbirth is. Don't remind them that that you have had a little experience yourself of giving birth; they're not going to believe you."

It's such a pity when parents like these are disappointed if their birth isn't straightforward, and they may even feel guilty if it involves drugs or a Caesarean. Surely what matters is the result, a beautiful, healthy baby? And that is the best comfort that grandmothers can provide.

Above all the baby represents something truly positive and life-affirming. It's almost like being reborn. Anxiety is invariably superseded by excitement, beginning with the first scan, showing the little dot that is your grandchild. Growing foetuses are invariably compared with fruit. First of all the little being is a peanut, then a lemon, then an apple. Once it's the size of a melon you find your legs are crossing as you remember your own pregnancy.

"Prepare for too much information," warns *Saga* magazine. "You will be shown dark swirly pictures which look less like a future grandchild and more like the satellite picture of a nasty storm building up over the Gulf of Mexico."

All of the grandmothers I spoke to overwhelmingly agreed that they felt very differently when their own daughter was having a baby. Tina admitted that while she adores all her grandchildren, she does feel closer to her daughter's three boys than to her son's little girl. "I'm working on it, though," she added.

Miranda already has three grandchildren, daughters of her two boys. But when her daughter became pregnant, her reaction was almost physical – as if she could feel the transformation herself. "I actually began to get her symptoms," she said. "I was sick when she was sick. I even thought my breasts were swelling, although my husband claimed he hadn't noticed."

"I was excited, of course," confided Judy. "But mainly I must admit I felt relieved. By the time my daughter became pregnant almost all my friends were on their second or third. So I was pleased that at last I could be part of that privileged gang."

Some women, though, may still be waiting, or know that they will never become grandmothers. So it can be painful for them when excited expectant grandmothers flaunt photos of the first scan, or ostentatiously brandish pregnancy magazines and baby patterns. Even the most generous friend who endlessly inquires about progress and wants to know every detail may feel understandably wistful, so it's important to be aware of their sensitivities.

You may choose to be present at the birth of a grandchild, and this can be a deeply rewarding experience, strengthening the bond between mother and daughter or daughter-in-law. Being a birth companion may involve just being there without doing much, or it may mean taking a more active part: back-rubbing, brow-soothing, making encouraging noises. Sometimes it's the father who may need reassurance and support.

But it's not always such a positive adventure. "We're a close family," confided Griselda, "so I found myself in the labour ward with my daughter, her husband and her sister, as well as the midwife. As they were all busily motivating her, comforting and encouraging, I sat at the business end feeling quite redundant. I suppose there were just too many of us, and I wondered what on earth I was doing there. Until the moment that the baby's head began to appear. Watching my granddaughter emerging from my own daughter was one of the most glorious and moving moments of my life. All my embarrassment evaporated and I was left with such a sense of joy and completion."

If your daughter is a single mother she's likely to want you to be with her for the birth. "I was a bit wary of being there," said Josie. "I worried that I might not be able to stand seeing her in pain. What if I fainted? But I was so glad we went through it together. It was almost as if we were both giving birth, both working together to produce my beautiful grandson. We're now a very bonded little trio."

And she'll need you for so much more than just the birth. A woman whose partner is no longer with her will look to her mother for the support she needs: someone to hold her hair during the first sickness months; a sympathetic ear for her anxieties; reassurance that the mood swings, the tears, the panics are perfectly normal as her hormones kick in; someone to share the magic landmarks; a companion for all the hospital visits.

Despite the sadness and anxiety that some families will face, for most grannies the excitement will grow with every stage of the pregnancy journey. By the third semester parents can learn the sex of their baby. Some decide they'd rather wait for the surprise. Others can't wait to spread the news. What matters is that they have the choice. I remember being outraged that the hospital knew before I did, and wouldn't tell me.

Nowadays, most parents relish announcing whether their coming baby is a girl or a boy, while some go even further by holding a gender-reveal party. These began to take hold about fifteen years ago in America, and developed into riotous events when couples would light pink or blue fireworks and serve gender-appropriate cakes. The practice began to die down after one enthusiastic California couple managed to set off a wildfire, and since then there have been several more. Many warn against assuming a child's sex and gender identity are one and the same. One couple, wishing not to fall foul of the trans community, simply held up a bottle of champagne and declared that their child was gender-fluid. The custom hasn't died out though. Last year the tennis star Serena Williams and her husband Alex held a gender-reveal party where they set off a blaze of pink fireworks spelling out the words "*It's a girl.*"

In the UK it's much more common for expectant mothers to hold baby showers – often with Granny holding pride of place. My daughter's friends organised a picnic where everyone brought not only gifts but tips and advice too, all bound in a book: invest in a white noise machine, stock up on muslin cloths, don't fall down the rabbit hole of "who's more tired …"

As the picnic was in a park with no available loos, I worried that my heavily pregnant daughter might be caught short, so I proudly flourished what I thought was a practical solution: a she-wee, a pink plastic device much used by festival-goers, which allows them to pee standing up. But I caused helpless laughter when I tried to demonstrate how to use it. Scarlett wisely refused to touch it, and resorted to the time-honoured method: she went behind a bush.

It's during that endless wait for the baby to appear that grandmothers begin to wonder what they'd like to be called. Will you be Grandma, Nana or Granny? Or how about these names from different languages?

Nonna (Italian)
Obaasan (Japanese)
Oma (German)
Vovo (Portuguese)
Babcia (Polish)
Abuela (Spanish)
Bubbe (Yiddish)
Yiayia (Greek)

Some women, like the actress Goldie Hawn, will reject any of the granny names as old-fashioned and derogatory. "Grandmother," she remarked in her memoir *A Lotus Grows in the Mud*, "is a word that had so many connotations of old age and decrepitude." So what was her alternative? "My son Oliver decided I should be called 'Glam-Ma,' which I thought was quite brilliant and made us all laugh so hard."

When Sarah Ferguson, Duchess of York, became a grandmother she declared that she'd prefer to be called Duchy instead of grandma. "Lots of my friends call me Duch, so I think it will end up being Duchy," she said. "I call myself Duchess Doodle because I'm always doodling." Susan Sarandon likes to be called Honey, while Labour MP Angela Rayner has chosen Grangela.

But whatever you decide, don't leave it until the baby is old enough to come up with a name for you itself. You won't want to be introduced at parties as Goo-Goo or, even worse, Ga-Ga. One granny I know is still called Googly, and has to suffer endless teasing during the Test Match.

After some pondering together with my daughter's mother-in-law we came up with a pleasing solution. She is Grandma, I'm Granny. Both fathers insist on being Grandad. No matter what we're called we, like you, are active, busy, doting, happily proud grandparents.

Butterfly Laughter
by Katherine Mansfield

In the middle of our porridge plates
There was a blue butterfly painted
And each morning we tried who should reach the
butterfly first.
Then the Grandmother said: "Do not eat the poor
butterfly."
That made us laugh.
Always she said it and always it started us laughing.
It seemed such a sweet little joke.
I was certain that one fine morning
The butterfly would fly out of our plates,
Laughing the teeniest laugh in the world,
And perch on the Grandmother's lap.

Two

Hello Stranger

At last! After that long wait the baby has arrived. Your love affair has begun, as Joanna Lumley vividly remembers. "I love being a grandmother," she declared "That feeling you have for your own child – you don't ever think it will be replicated … But my heart was taken on day one."

Once you've heard the news it's natural to want to rush to the bedside with flowers and champagne and adorable outfits. Many grandmothers will want to be on hand to feed the exhausted parents and give them sleep breaks. But they may not be welcome. Some couples decide they'd rather have no visitors at all. They want time to get to know the baby and to become a family. This "babymoon" is quite a new invention and does make a lot of sense, but it can also be hurtful for disappointed grandmothers.

"Son and daughter-in-law have indicated they want a week to bond on their own and get into a routine," one wrote to the website Gransnet. "I knew they didn't want lots of visitors after the birth but didn't dream this meant grandparents too."

On the other hand, many new mothers welcome the help and encouragement you can provide. "My mother was the perfect grandmother," one grateful woman remembered. "I took care of the baby and she ran the support system. She did the shopping and the cooking and she kept the house going. She also made me feel pretty special. It even beats cooking to have somebody with you who's warm and affectionate and supportive."

It's tempting to want to pass on your own experience to a new parent. When Meryl Streep discovered her daughter was going to have a baby, she announced happily, "I'm going to go out and ruin her life. I specialise in unsolicited advice."

After all, we've been there and done that and so have a wealth of wisdom to impart. But advice isn't always welcome, and it isn't necessarily right, either. New grandmothers quickly learn how much has changed.

Parents in the early 1950s would faithfully follow the rules of the New Zealand child development expert Truby King. He advocated strict routines, leaving the baby outside for an hour a day, limiting cuddles and feeding every four hours, ignoring any crying. This is how many of today's grandmothers were raised. Those of us who worked on *Woman's Hour* were convinced that the programme was scheduled at two in the afternoon because that was when mothers throughout the land would be feeding. That, we liked to think, was a handy way to pass on feminism through breast milk.

At around the same time a far kinder approach was advocated by Dr Spock. "Trust yourself. You know more than you think you do," he advised. "Parenting is about choices and deciding what's best for your child." His teachings were a welcome relief from Truby King's authoritarian methods, and made way for Penelope Leach, who was the childcare guru for many of today's grandparents and is still very influential. She believed that leaving a child to cry was damaging, and that you should practise "Controlled Comforting" – going back to the crying baby every three minutes.

So it's best to avoid that hazardous phrase "In my day." Today's parents face a welter of conflicting theories and strategies, from books and programmes to online chat rooms and social media platforms. Grandmothers would do well to recognise that they may sometimes be out of date.

Swaddling, for example, drifts in and out of fashion. Some grandmothers may swear by it, arguing that tiny babies feel more secure when tightly wrapped. Others, from a different generation, are horrified by the idea, concerned that the baby may overheat or suffocate. "My daughters-in-law perceived swaddling as verging on the barbaric so I never got to repeat the experience with my grandchildren," one woman wrote to Gransnet. "They also torched my suggestion that their babies should be put outside in the pram for their daytime naps, on the grounds that the babies may feel abandoned. So I quietly crawled back into my shell and just smiled in a granny kind of way."

Sleep is another disputed area. About 30 years ago, when grandmothers were having their own children, babies had to be put on their sides, to guard against cot deaths. Current advice is to lie them on their backs – which will appal grandmothers who had been warned that this might cause choking.

Today's mothers seem alarmingly well informed, and can baffle you with new ideas and even new terms. You may never have heard of "four-month sleep regression", for example. At four months, it seems, babies tend to forget any established routine and parents have to learn all over again how to get them to sleep. If in despair, they will turn to a sleep consultant – another recent development – who will recommend a strict, exactly timed regime that usually does the trick. It means that parents will become slaves to the timetable. But at least it will work – until the next regression.

Then there's the fraught business of breast-feeding. "Breast is best" was a mantra for my generation of mothers. At a time when the natural childbirth movement was beginning to emerge, we recoiled from the idea of formula milk. Why replace our own good milk with a powdered substitute? Especially as many of us could still remember the Ostermilk our own mothers fed us.

Most mothers still believe that breast-feeding is best for the baby – and much cheaper than any commercial product. But there are often good reasons why this isn't possible, and it's so unfair if mothers who can't manage it are made to feel inadequate. Many will struggle on determinedly, despite the frustrations when a baby just can't latch on, or when nipples become unbearably sore. This is when your support and reassurance will be crucial.

Mothers who are having trouble in the first weeks will often express their milk so that the baby will still benefit from the nourishment. I used to use a plastic pump which probably should have been consigned to a museum of torture. These implements have been replaced by much more efficient electronic devices, which will usually be supplied by the hospital. Very often, expressing will help with the transition from bottle to breast, and babies usually get the hang of it after a couple of months.

Help is also at hand from another recently discovered technique, whereby the desperate mother is encouraged to lie naked on the bed with the baby on her stomach. The idea is that the closeness and warmth will encourage the milk to flow, and draw the baby to the nipple.

Even the most familiar aspects of baby care have changed since your own children were born. You may think you know how to change a nappy, for example – but watch your son or daughter doing it before you have a go. They will have their own routine, and will be insistent on their own brands of creams and nappies.

Nappies today are easier to use than they used to be. The sticky tapes actually stick, and they're designed so that the baby won't feel uncomfortable when they're wet. Some of you will have stark memories of using the old cloth versions: the stinging jabs of safety pins, the leaks, the rashes, that distinctive odour of ammonia? Well, all that is back with a vengeance, thanks to environmentally conscious parents who, to avoid building acres of landfill, will choose terry nappies. If you really want to help them, the best present you can possibly give is a subscription to a nappy service. It will save them hours of boiling and drying, and there will be no unsightly piles cluttering up the kitchen.

Some grandparents are so overwhelmed by their new responsibilities that they join grandparenting classes, just to be sure they're doing it right. Happy Parents, Happy Baby, for example, claims to provide "all the latest guidelines for caring for a baby, including safe sleep and feeding; baby first aid; washing and dressing, nappy changing, feeding, settling a baby; and baby safety." The Baby Experience offers workshops on Zoom, covering sleep training, feeding, bathing, babywear and how to understand the baby brain.

Writing in *The Observer*, Eva Wiseman was baffled that anyone would need to learn the obvious. "Turns out, they're a whole thing. Grantenatal classes cost around £40 a session (though I hear rumours of a course that costs £300 – I guess this is for luxury babies) … Do they learn, I wondered, how to offer 16 desserts a day? Do they learn how to secrete tissues in their sleeve?" But Eva does recognise that these preparations can have their uses. "The anxiety around parenting is not limited to those approaching it for the first time – instead this fear can linger and mutate. So if a class gives someone more confidence to grandparent happily, then I'm in. After all, these are the people keeping our families upright. The true test is in dealing with these dickheads they raised first time round."

Even though these courses can be reassuring, they can't possibly cover every anxiety, or every opportunity for grandparents to go wrong. Some parents, for example, are wary about exposing their children to the public gaze, or feel uncomfortable about grandparents' obsessive need to share photos, especially now that their precious newborn will be ogled by strangers via Instagram and Facebook. In her book *Becoming a Grandmother* the childcare expert Sheila Kitzinger quotes a woman who complained that her mother-in-law only came round to take photographs. "She doesn't do anything to help. I can be working myself into the ground and she is there with her camera. She wants snaps to show her friends."

So beware of boasting, even if you're unlikely to go quite as far as the actress Gina Lollobrigida, who went a little overboard when she became a grandmother. "Full of pride, she wanted to present him in the grandiose style she has grown accustomed to," gushed *Hello* magazine, alongside photographs of the star in three costume changes, posing in the garden with her four-month-old grandson.

Once the child arrives it's tempting to shower her with gifts. But this, too, can be tricky. Baby clothes, even for newborns, are all too often designated by gender: pink for a girl, blue for a boy. Grannies who love to prettify little girls with frilly dresses and bows on their heads may not be thanked by parents hoping to avoid the stereotypes.

New-wave feminists despair of the way toys are still colour-coded – just as we thought we'd moved on. In a recent *New York Times* article, *Ms.* magazine's family editor, Cottin Pogrebin, explained her disappointment. "Now I have a stroke when I go through toy stores where still everything is pink and blue. When you order a toy online, they say, 'Is it for a girl or a boy?' They don't say, 'Is this a child who's interested in nature or in bugs or in dinosaurs?' They say, 'Boy or girl?' That was gone in the '70s and '80s. But that's all slid backwards."

One gift that will certainly be appreciated is baby equipment. You might be surprised by the amount of paraphernalia that a newborn needs these days. There's so much choice that it's best to let the parents select what they need. That task is usually left to fathers – who may not make the most practical decisions. My nephew Andrew bought a sturdy-looking car seat to take his son home from hospital, but it was so complicated to fix that he had to call on a fellow dad, plus hospital porter, to put it together. The equally safe-looking buggy that Sam chose for his daughter turned out to be too heavy to lift on to the bus. Do watch out, though, if the proud parents hanker after one of those contraptions that are pram, pushchair and car seat all-in-one. Top-of-the range ones will cost well over £1000!

You could avoid all traps by just giving money. It may not be romantic, but a contribution to a baby ISA tends to be hugely appreciated – and it's gender-neutral.

If your daughter is a single parent she'll be far more likely to rely on you for help during those early months. If the father of the baby is no longer there, she may well expect you to take his place. Who else would be there to share her frustration when the baby won't feed, or won't stop crying, or when she just so desperately needs to sleep?

There are so many different kinds of families these days: nuclear, single-parent, same-sex, families where different generations live together, blended families where the children may be step- or half-siblings, mixed-race or mixed-religion families. Many rejoice in their differences, delighting in learning about new cultures and traditions, as I've so often witnessed at the ceremonies I conduct as a humanist celebrant.

The father of the new little boy at one of my baby namings came from a Muslim family. At the end of the ceremony his father stepped forward and took his grandson in his arms to recite a blessing for him. The whole room erupted into cheers.

But nothing can beat the sheer joyful eclecticism described by American Indian writer Bharati Mukherjee, of Hindu origin. She was attending the baby naming for her Chinese granddaughter, adopted by her American son Bart and his wife Kimberly Ann. A statue of Buddha smiled over the gathering, and following a traditional Chinese game, a toy medical kit, a pen and a ten-dollar bill were used to predict the little girl's future. If the baby chose the money she'd become a businesswoman; if the pen, a scholar; if the medical equipment, she'd be a doctor. Dinner was served in a Bengali restaurant, although Brahmins are forbidden to eat food cooked by a Muslim. Sunday brunch next day was from yet another culture: lox and bagels.

When I conduct mixed weddings I always relish the vivid exchanges of traditions. At one, the congregation joined in a hearty rendition of "Jerusalem" just before the bridegroom stamped on a glass in true Jewish fashion. At another, a strapping blond Danish groom married his tiny Sikh bride. Everyone had joined in merrily with the party the night before, so at the ceremony itself all the Viking-like women proudly flaunted their beautifully hennaed hands, alongside their delighted in-laws.

But differences in religion can also lead to friction. Mary was appalled when her Jewish son-in-law insisted that the new little boy be circumcised. "I couldn't believe he was prepared to mutilate my perfect little grandson with such a barbaric, outmoded ritual," she said. But after some fraught conversations she came to realise how deeply embedded and important the practice is to religious Jews, so, to keep the peace, she reluctantly attended the *briss*. Although at the crucial wielding of the knife she fainted.

One secular granny told me how uncomfortable she feels that her Catholic daughter-in-law takes her child to Mass every week and plans to send her to a faith school. "It's just indoctrination," she frets. "Why can't she make up her own mind?" Of course, eventually she will decide for herself. So, as always, the wisest course of action is to take no action at all. It's a grandmother's duty to stifle her disapproval.

Increasingly, women who realise they may never find a suitable partner but desperately long for a baby will go ahead alone, by resorting to a sperm bank. That doesn't always go down well with the rest of the family. "My parents are devout Christians," said Pauline, "and they profoundly disapprove of the choice I've made. Now that Jack is here, my mother is making quite an effort to accept him. But my father still refuses to see Jack. It breaks my heart that he'll never get to know his grandfather."

When Amanda decided to use a sperm bank she was very much alone, as both her parents had died. The baby naming was tinged with sadness. But here are the promises she made to him on that day. "What I truly wish for him is a life full of love. I hope he grows to be a kind and compassionate man; a man who knows himself, his likes and dislikes, and who can stand his ground without pushing people aside. And I want more than anything for the choices that I've made not to define his self-worth, or be a label, but something to be celebrated and, well, just normal."

That's how many families will see it – welcoming the new addition and offering nothing but support to the mother. "When I made the decision, my mother couldn't have been more delighted," Charlotte said. "She already had three grandchildren and couldn't wait for another. She and my sister were so much more experienced than me, I relied on them to be my steering group. And although Rex doesn't have a daddy, he does have a wonderful extended family, with three cousins who adore him."

When Libby and her partner Alison decided to create a family with donated sperm, Alison went first, and had a little girl. Two years later Libby gave birth to their son – using the same donor. Now the whole family is living happily with Supergran – Libby's mum Lucy.

One of my most moving ceremonies was for a little boy called Joel. Marcus and Genista had been friends since their schooldays and both had separately found themselves contemplating if, when and how they might become parents. As Genista didn't have a partner she decided to go ahead alone with a sperm donation, but was adamant that her child must know its father, who would play an active role in his or her life. Marcus, who is gay, feared he might not ever become a father, but if that was possible he'd want a great relationship with his child's mother and extended family.

Eventually, after much discussion, they decided to have that baby together – and they created something of a blueprint for how all parenting should be. They devised a contract covering every contingency, from schooling to meals to toys. And, most of all, their shared values. "Our mutual goals for the child are to provide a stable, nurturing environment, a good education, love, affection and commitment. We will seek to help our child meet their full potential, encourage creativity, intellectual, emotional and social growth."

All through that ceremony two women were quietly sobbing with joy. They were, of course, the two grandmothers, neither of whom had dreamed that this day would ever come. I've never forgotten the overflowing love of that gathering and the warm acceptance of such an unconventional family. They seemed to me a symbol of hope for all the different models of parents and families who make up today's multifaceted world.

All of the women I've met who have conceived in this way are determined that their child should know who the father is and where they came from. Some choose to use Danish sperm banks where it's legal for children to trace their biological fathers; in the UK, they can only do this if the donor has agreed to remove his anonymity. But in the United States there's very little regulation, which means there's no limit on how many children a donor might father. When she was in her 20s Chrysta Bilton discovered that her father Jeffrey Harris had been a serial donor, and she could have hundreds of siblings.

That's one worry that grannies in the UK don't have to face. But there is another vexed area of disagreement that is causing increasing anguish. "I'm appalled that my daughter is refusing to have her new baby vaccinated," said Sandra, one desperate grandmother. "What's so frustrating is her nonchalance about her decision. It's almost like wilful ignorance." She's not alone. It's estimated that one in seven children will now start primary school without having been given vaccines, leaving them vulnerable to dangerous diseases like measles and polio. Measles is now on the rise, although in 2018 the UK had eliminated the disease. In January 2024 the NHS launched a publicity campaign after figures showed there had been about 250 confirmed measles cases in England during the previous year. Most were in children under 10 years old.

Vaccination rates have dropped to about 85 per cent nationally, and far lower in parts of London, according to UK Health Security Agency chief executive Jenny Harries. That is "too low to maintain safe population coverage," she said. "We want that at about 95 per cent as advised by the

World Health Organisation." Public health officials say more than 3.4 million children under 16 years old are unprotected and at risk of catching preventable diseases.

The increase in vaccine hesitancy was prompted by Dr Andrew Wakefield's claim, in 1978, that there was a link between the combined measles, mumps, rubella (MMR) vaccine and subsequent development of colitis and autism. Although Wakefield's theory has been widely discredited, many people continue to believe it and mistrust the advice of doctors and other health experts.

So what can grandparents like Sandra do to persuade their children to change their minds? First of all, don't rush to criticise them. That may only cause resentment and hostility. Instead, discuss the matter with them as calmly as you can, listen to their reasons and try to understand, before attempting to dissuade them. Let them know that you are as concerned for their children's health and welfare as they are, so you are both on the same side rather than adversaries.

Some parents simply want more information before they are satisfied that inoculation is really safe. There are those who question whether these powerful vaccines are administered too early. Others are worried about the multiple contents of today's vaccines. They would like to know more about their possible effects. "Some of the contents are actually poisonous," one father said. "You really wouldn't want mercury or aluminium in a tiny baby, even if the quantities are very small."

If they are open to discussion, simply counteract their arguments with the facts. Vaccines will protect your child from contracting these horrible diseases. They will also prevent them from spreading. You could point out that measles is now on the increase again, because of the number of children who are not inoculated.

Many of today's grandparents will remember the terror of the polio outbreak in the 1950s. Children who contracted polio would often become paralysed, as the disease affects the spinal cord. Polio too had been eliminated in the UK but there is serious concern that it may be returning. After poliovirus was detected last year in sewage in north and east London, the NHS offered a booster vaccine dose for young children.

Some people just won't accept how dangerous these illnesses are, even if you point out that measles and meningitis can lead to brain damage or even death, while mumps and meningitis can cause permanent deafness. Committed anti-vaxers may not agree.

"My son and daughter-in-law live a very alternative lifestyle, where they believe that a natural approach is safest," confided Susan, another worried grandmother. "Like many of their friends, they just think all these warnings are exaggerated scare stories. They maintain that as long as their children eat healthy food and live a natural life that won't overburden the immune system, they won't get ill. I just see all this as ludicrous hippy claptrap, but when I confront them they think I'm attacking them."

Even more worrying, some actually believe that contracting one of these diseases could be good for their children, giving them immunity. It's an argument that became common during the Covid-19 pandemic, when some experts advocated a policy of herd immunity. But the comparison just doesn't hold up. Covid can of course be debilitating, and deadly to some vulnerable people, but it's not on the same scale as the vaccine-related childhood illnesses that cause permanent damage and even death.

All you can do, if your arguments are ignored, is hope that these vaccine hesitants will eventually realise the hazards they are exposing their children to. Or you may be able to identify a relative or friend whom they trust and admire, and see if they might be more successful.

*

Within the maelstrom of anxiety, delight and excitement that every grandmother feels when a new baby arrives, her overriding emotion will be, quite simply, huge pride and happiness. And there will be new decisions to make.

Once they know their baby's sex, parents can start deciding on a name. That, too, can be a source of concern to grannies. A 2017 Mumsnet and Gransnet survey of over 2,000 grandparents revealed that a fifth said they hated their grandchild's name, and 15 per cent said it sounded "made-up" or unconventional. Grandmothers had stronger views on their grandchildren's names than grandfathers, with 44 per cent of parents reporting that complaints came from their own mother, and 42 per cent from their mother-in-law.

Wise grannies will try not to comment. Even if you're unhappy about the chosen name, try to sport a bland smile for little Arsenal, raise a proud cheer for baby Nintendo. My daughter Scarlett wouldn't reveal the name of her coming daughter, but did offer a clue: it was connected with *Game of Thrones*. So there were a few awkward moments when we contemplated calling out to Daenerys, or practised letting

Targaryen roll off the tongue. Fortunately, she's called Emilia. Phew!

Many families choose to welcome a new baby with a christening or a similar religious ceremony, but increasingly couples prefer something non-religious, like the namings that I perform. These are wonderfully inclusive occasions – a chance to bring the families together and to mark the uniqueness of the new addition. Guests may be asked to write wishes or advice, to be hung on a tree or pinned to a board. Some parents distribute seeds for people to plant in honour of the baby. One couple went further, and planted a tree in soil nourished by the placenta.

I'm always moved by the love and warmth of these events. Here's the wish one woman made to her little granddaughter:

My wish for you, Amelia,
is that you will smile the brightest smile,
Be happy most of the time,
Feel brave, feel strong,
Be healthy and live long,
Run along windy beaches,
Climb trees to far off reaches,
Feel the sun and smell the rain,
Pick blackberries on a country lane,
I wish you love and laughter and lots of fun,
I wish your life and dreams to be full of sun.

Another grandmother spoke of her own delight.

The joy of seeing you – your smiles, your laughter, your wonder at the world, drinking it all (in) and learning, learning… . Every day a blessing and my heart fills with pride and happiness – "so special". I feel honoured to be sharing your lives and your first small steps in this world … your world. I wish you well on your journeys and will always love you…

After the excitement, the parties, the gifts, the gushing, comes the next crucial step: getting to know your grandchild. You'll melt when the tiny baby clutches your finger, when those huge, trusting eyes gaze into your face. And nothing can quite prepare you for the radiant frisson of that first, precious smile. But very soon the baby will begin to develop a personality – and that's when you'll need to perfect the art of becoming the best ever grandmother.

That's much easier to do if you live nearby and see your grandchild regularly. But grannies who visit less frequently could be in for a shock after the first few months. The baby may suddenly turn away from you, crying even when you come near. You so badly want to bond with her, but when you try to hold her those cries turn into shrieks.

However rejected you may feel, her reaction doesn't mean that she doesn't like you. It's just that she doesn't recognise you, so sees you as a stranger. Babies are naturally conservative creatures. They don't like change. Especially any change to their safe world.

At about eight months old babies develop what is known as "separation anxiety" – when they realise how dependent they are on their closest people. Consequently they don't feel safe without them. They will become clingy, crying if their parent leaves the room.

It's better to avoid taking your grandchild out of a parent's arms – especially if you notice the baby is pulling back or turning away. You might try to talk softly and hold out your hands to her. But don't be too upset if she won't come to you. When my granddaughter started to become clingy and anxious, I soon learned not to try to hold her. Instead I'd sit on the floor with her and play. But even if her mother moved out of sight across the kitchen she'd start her pitiful, abandoned weeping.

"I was so upset when my grandson suddenly wouldn't let me hold him," confided Angela. "I tried holding out my arms to him, stroking him while he was in my daughter's arms, but he'd just turn his head away. I decided to ignore him at first when I visited. I'd pick up one of his toys and start playing with it, and eventually he would crawl over to join me. It was a start."

"I couldn't understand why the baby would happily settle with her childminder – but never with me," confided Sunita, another disappointed granny. "So I tried another method. I'd offer to take her for a walk in her pushchair. Once we were off she'd soon forget that she'd left her mum behind."

This seems to be the answer. Babies have very short memories. That's why they won't remember you if they don't see you every day. But it also means that once their mother or father is out of the way, they'll quickly forget about them. Most of the grandmothers I spoke to agreed that if they were left in sole charge of the grandchild the tears and clinginess would soon evaporate.

Remember that even if it takes time, this stage will pass. My granddaughter is now perfectly happy to be alone with me. Clinginess is just a passing phase, those early anxieties fading as children adapt to their new world, and begin to understand that just because their parents are out of sight, it doesn't mean that they are gone for ever. By this time your baby grandchild will have morphed into a charming, funny, tantrummy, highly opinionated and totally unpredictable new being. In other words – a toddler.

He will proudly take his first unsteady steps, a bit like an unguided robot as he chases after pigeons in the park. With each small triumph – climbing the stairs, braving the slide, uttering those first stumbling words – the bond will begin to fuse. Very soon you'll become a top favourite. "Alexa, get Granny on the phone," three-year-old Iris will order the device. "I want to Facetime Nana," Hari will announce.

From now on you can look forward to a galaxy of adventures. You're going to become an expert in everything from *Peppa Pig* to dinosaurs; you'll relish that cuddle on your lap as you read the same story over and over again, with little Marmitey fingers jabbing at the pages. Everything from rainbows and snow to bulldozers and giraffes in the zoo will shine with magic, as if you're experiencing it for the first time. As you view the world with that new sense of wonder, you really will feel as if you have been born again.

Poem for a Daughter

By Anne Stevenson

'I think I'm going to have it,'
I said, joking between pains.
The midwife rolled competent
sleeves over corpulent milky arms.
'Dear, you never have it,
we deliver it.'
A judgement the years proved true.
Certainly I've never had you

as you still have me, Caroline.
Why does a mother need a daughter?
Heart's needle, hostage to fortune,
freedom's end. Yet nothing's more perfect
than that bleating, razor-shaped cry
that delivers a mother to her baby.
The bloodcord snaps that held
their sphere together. The child,
tiny and alone, creates the mother.

A woman's life is her own
until it is taken away
by a first particular cry.
Then she is not alone
but a part of the premises
of everything there is:
a time, a tribe, a war.
When we belong to the world
we become what we are.

Three

Hard Times

Grandmothers will always fear that something might go wrong. So how do you support the mother through a miscarriage, or if the baby doesn't survive? In the past, miscarriages were rarely discussed. When my own mother came home from hospital without a baby, no one even mentioned it. She was not alone. Miscarriages used to be a dark secret, best buried. Hospitals would simply dispose of the foetus without the parents even seeing him or her.

These days, though, there is much more understanding of the parents' shock and grief, the mother's distraught agony exacerbated by her raging hormones. From the very start of a pregnancy the dreams and the plans begin, the assumption that a new member of the family is on the way. So when no baby arrives, all of those fantasies are shattered.

It's usual now for the parents to be given the baby to hold, to cuddle, to have the reassurance that, however briefly, this was their child and they were parents. The anxious grandmother will be deeply affected too. The death of a baby will feel to her like an offence against nature, like breaking off a bud before it has had a chance to flower. But however deep her pain, her responsibility now is to be there to support, to comfort, to do what she has always done. To try to make everything better.

Talking about the experience can be very healing. When Chrissy Telgen and her husband, the musician and producer John Legend, lost their baby at 20 weeks, she decided to make her grief public, even publishing photographs of the stillborn child. She felt compelled to share one of the worst experiences of her life because, sadly, 10 to 20 per cent of known pregnancies end in miscarriage.

"We are shocked and in the kind of deep pain you only hear about, the kind of pain we've never felt before," she said. "We were never able to stop the bleeding and give our baby the fluids he needed, despite bags and bags of blood transfusions. It just wasn't enough. We never decide on our babies' names until the last possible moment after they're born, just before we leave the hospital. But we, for some reason, had started to call this little guy in my belly Jack. So he will always be Jack to us. Jack worked so hard to be a part of our little family, and he will be, forever. To our Jack—I'm so sorry that the first few moments of your life were met with so many complications, that we couldn't give you the home you needed to survive. We will always love you."

Since her revelation, she has received a flood of support from so many parents, thanking her for her courage and sharing their own miscarriage experiences.

With a late miscarriage or stillbirth, parents often choose to hold a funeral for the baby – to acknowledge his or her existence, and to say farewell in the presence of loving family and friends. As a humanist celebrant I have conducted quite a few of these. They are always heartbreaking. Yet even while the sobbing parents carry in the tiny coffin, soft music murmuring grief, inadequate words reaching out to share their sorrow, I'm always aware that there is some comfort in these simple ceremonies.

Sometimes, a grandmother will be asked to say a few words or to read a poem. More often, though, she'll just be there: a strong, steady symbol of reassurance. It's at difficult times that the granny is most needed, most able to bring the comfort that only she can provide.

What is most important is hope – hope for recovery, for a future new life, and for the joys to come.

Many women have trouble conceiving a baby in the first place. Going through the agonies of infertility can be a long and frustrating journey. Although treatment has vastly improved, the process of IVF is still unpredictable and many women have had to endure endless disappointments as each month brings fresh hope and renewed despair. If you are living through this fraught time with your daughter or daughter-in-law you may be as anxious as she is. But however much you long for that grandchild, do try not to let your own feelings show. That will just add more pressure, and sometimes more guilt, too.

It's quite common for women to feel tearful or anxious after giving birth. This sensation is known as the "baby blues" and it doesn't usually last for more than a couple of weeks. But if the symptoms persist, or start later, the mother may be suffering from postnatal depression. Sometimes she may not even realise that this is what is happening to her, and it may not have occurred to others either. So do be vigilant if something seems wrong with your daughter or daughter-in-law. Perhaps she seems continually sad and listless, unable to enjoy herself and with little interest in what is going on around her. She may avoid contact with other people, and have trouble sleeping. Even more worrying, she may find it difficult to cope with the baby.

Everything seemed to be fine at first when Susanna had her first baby. But after about a month her mother Jacqueline noticed that things weren't quite right. "She was quiet, something was withheld. It was like she was behind a glass screen," Jacqueline told *Good Housekeeping*. "We went out for a coffee and she was slightly on edge about the baby crying, and whether people would be irritated by that."

Once she realised that something was wrong, Jacqueline went to the doctor with her daughter. That's when it became clear how ill Susanna was. She was immediately admitted to hospital.

Jacqueline describes her most difficult moment as when she visited Susanna at the hospital mental health unit where she was receiving treatment. "We went to visit her with her husband and the baby. Seeing her there, somewhere with secure doors – that was pretty scary. She's still my baby, so having to leave her there at the end of visiting time, taking her baby with me, was pretty upsetting."

While not everyone going through PND is treated at hospital, that was deemed the best care option for Susanna. "Just after she came out of hospital, the baby gave a little smile and I've got a photograph of Susanna smiling back at her. That was lovely to see, that relationship between them – Susanna's unguarded smile back at her looked exactly as it should be."

She added, "My husband and I are so proud of her, as our daughter and as a mum."

It can be really helpful to accompany your daughter to medical appointments, said Jacqueline, especially if the condition is so severe that she can't talk. You can then answer questions for her, as well as offering her the companionship she needs so that she doesn't feel so alone.

There's still a lot of prejudice or misunderstanding about this frightening condition. Jacqueline believes there needs to be much more open discussion about it, and more advice for pregnant women and new mothers. "You might need postnatal exercises to get back into shape, and you also might need some help with your mental health because you've gone through such a huge change," she says. "Postnatal depression is no different from when you're pregnant and you've got extremely high blood pressure. There's nothing a mother can do about either. But in some people's minds there's this idea that people should somehow be able to pull themselves out of PND."

The charity PANDAS, specialising in advice about postnatal depression, encourages grandparents to find out all they can about the condition so that they can offer the most appropriate support. Practical tasks like bringing food, cooking, washing and shopping will help to lift the dark burden oppressing the poor mother. Let her know it's okay to talk about how she's feeling, so she'll know you're listening with quiet, undemanding sympathy.

As a grandmother you will need to muster even more strength and resilience if the child is born with a disability. Grandparents experience a "double grief" when this happens: they are not only grieving for the grandchild, but for their own child and their lost dreams.

"As a grandparent, you may find yourself in an unfamiliar and sometimes difficult situation," according to the charity Contact in its *Guide for Grandparents*. "The child's parents, siblings and other relatives may look to you for information and support at a time when you are trying to come to terms with the news that your grandchild has a disability."

They quote one grandmother describing her feelings when she heard the news. "It was hard coping and fighting. If only I was ten years younger. I was very angry. Why our boy? It was hard to know how to support my daughter and her husband – I tried to give them space. It was very difficult to accept. I wanted to do more to help. It was a double whammy – concerned for the child's parents but also worried about the child."

"Whether a child is born with a disability or becomes disabled later in life, their needs will likely change the whole family," agrees Kerry Thompson, a disability blogger. "And grandparents are no exception. In fact, they can play a vital role in providing support for their adult children and care for their grandchildren."

"Do some research," urges Kerry, as "the more knowledge you have the better." She recommends that you do all you can to learn about the baby's condition. That way, you'll be better equipped to help as the child develops: understanding the needs of an autistic child, dealing with epileptic seizures, manipulating the wheelchair, becoming expert at administering medicine or physiotherapy.

Contact agrees that the first step to being a skilful grandparent to a child with a disability is being informed about their diagnosis and condition. By taking the time to understand the effect their disability will have on their life, you can be ready to be an integral part of that life yourself. You will be able to help care for them, support them, offer aid to the parents, and in some small way understand the difficulties such a disability presents to the child.

When Leila's child was born with epilepsy, reports Contact's *Guide*, the grandparents went straight to the internet and libraries for information about the disorder. They now know what needs to be done if the child has a seizure. It has given Leila and her husband a lot of comfort to know that her parents can handle Clare in an emergency when they visit them.

Although it may be daunting at first, one of the most vital supports you can offer is practical help with the specific needs of the child. Learn to manipulate a wheelchair, administer feeding tubes, give massages, help with reading or speaking. That way you'll develop a closer relationship with your grandchild, and be better equipped to offer warmth and love as she or he struggles with their condition.

Don't forget that the child's parents need support, too. Parents of special needs kids have an extremely high divorce rate because of the everyday stress and strain. Your son or daughter may need a friendly ear or a shoulder to cry upon. Or they may just need time off. So find time to look after the child, or offer to help with household chores. They'll hugely appreciate it if you can babysit, allowing them the chance to go out as a couple.

They often have to engage with formidable arrays of paperwork and bureaucracy to access the help they need. That's where you can step in, by becoming a fighting granny. When Carol's granddaughter was diagnosed with a learning difficulty, she took on the responsibility of negotiating with the local authority to get special needs support. "It was such a frustrating battle," she told me. "I got my way because they could tell I just wouldn't give up. But the last thing my poor daughter needed was yet more stress at such a distressing time."

Practical support can be hugely helpful – but emotional support may be even more important, according to disability blogger Emma. "I think it's important for grandparents to be there as much as possible, both physically and emotionally, for the parents and children. Sometimes emotional support can be more helpful, depending on the circumstances, as some days are harder than others. Most importantly, don't treat them differently because of their disability. Treat and love them unconditionally like any other child. And ultimately have fun and create wonderful memories the whole family can cherish."

Welcoming the child into the family can bring rewards to the grandparents, too. When her grandson Owen was diagnosed with Down Syndrome, Patty's first thoughts were for Owen's parents Sara and Mike. "What should have been a time of joy and excitement became a time of fear and helplessness," Patty wrote on the website for NADS (National Association for Down Syndrome). "All I knew was how much we had all loved Owen since the minute he was born. I turned to them and said, 'Just because someone came in here and put a label on him does not change who he is! Do not let that label define him. His name is OWEN! It is not Down syndrome!'

"I now watch with so much pride as this loving family grows together. Of course there are struggles! It is so hard not to worry. What will the future bring? What will the best education options be for him? Will he get a job? Will he live on his own? I try to encourage them to live in the moment.

"To me, Owen is just like most five-month-old babies! He loves to have people play on the floor with him during tummy time. He smiles, babbles and blows bubbles at us. He enjoys having books read to him and songs sung to him. He loves to put everything in his mouth. Owen has developed a personality all his own! If he is in a cranky mood and I sing 'You Are My Sunshine' to him, he stops crying or fussing and smiles. Oh how this little man can melt my heart!

"Owen Michael has blessed our family and filled me with hope. I have seen so much change in awareness and acceptance in the past 40 years of working with individuals with disabilities. I look at Owen and know he can teach others what it means to have different abilities. He will show all of us that the sky is the limit!"

Contact has found that most grandparents felt that having a disabled child in the family had helped them to be more understanding and to learn more about disability. One grandparent said that having a disabled grandchild had brought the whole family closer.

The best advice is the simplest: love your grandchild unconditionally and reap all the benefits of a close, loving relationship with the child and the whole family.

Your most important role, agrees Colleen Brosnan, the mother of two disabled children, is simply to "love your grandchild as they are, warts and all. Grandparents are lucky to be the ones who can embrace their child as they are – take advantage of it! Your grandchild will truly bask in your unconditional love."

Helga
by Carl Sandburg

The wishes on this child's mouth
Came like snow on marsh cranberries;
The tamarack kept something for her;
The wind is ready to help her shoes.
The north has loved her; she will be
A grandmother feeding geese on frosty
Mornings; she will understand
Early snow on the cranberries
Better and better then.

Four

Spoiling

"I know he's spoiled rotten," declared Joan Rivers. "I couldn't care less."

She wasn't alone. Many women take it for granted that they have a right to indulge their grandchildren. After all, they've done the hard job of bringing up their own children. So they welcome the chance to sit back and enjoy them, without having to lay down all those rules.

The idea that children can be "spoiled" has a long history, going back to the Bible, with the declaration in Proverbs that "He that spares his rod, hates his son." Embedded in the Protestant ethic is the view that children are innately sinful and must be held in check and disciplined, in the name of morality and health. So it began to be believed that a lack of harshness with children was to be regarded as "spoiling".

But why is it always grannies who get the blame for spoiling? This accusation was first made by the social scientist Hermann Vollmer. "Grandmothers exert an extraordinarily pernicious influence on their grandchildren," he claimed in his influential 1937 article "The Grandmother: a Problem in Childrearing". "The grandmother is not a suitable custodian of the care and rearing of her grandchild: she is a disturbing factor against which we are obligated to protect the child according to the best of our ability."

Today's grandmothers would be justifiably outraged at such an accusation. No wonder it's been roundly discredited as old-fashioned and misogynistic, especially now that the importance of grandmothers and their crucial contribution to family life is so widely recognised. Yet the image of the spoiling grandmother does seem to persist. A recent headline in the *Daily Mail* warned, "Parents are being 'run ragged' by their children when they get back from their grandparents because they've been so spoilt."

It referred to a study of 2,000 parents which found that 83 per cent say their children are regularly spoilt by their grandparents, with chocolate or cakes the most common treat. A third of parents claimed that their children are allowed to stay up past their bedtime at their grandparents' and get away with not eating any of their lunch or dinner.

It's still assumed that the chief culprit when it comes to spoiling is, of course, the grandmother. After all, many grandmothers see it as part of their job to give children what they're not allowed at home. But there's a danger that their permissiveness may undermine the authority of the parents. Indeed, Freud once suggested that the special bond between grandparents and children is that they are united against a common enemy: the parent. So when children are given whatever is forbidden at home they're conspiring with Granny in a kind of joint naughtiness.

"You know, the nice thing about being a grandmother is that you can spoil them occasionally," agreed Camilla, the Duchess of Cornwall. "Give them more of the things that their parents forbid them to have."

"I love my grannie Sarah best of everyone," announced three-year-old Ruby. "Because she gives me lots and lots of sweeties. And chocolates."

As you can imagine, Ruby's mum isn't quite as delighted. When she asked her mother-in-law to cut down on the treats, Sarah was genuinely shocked. For her, sweets are a major way of showing love. Like many grandmothers, she remembers her own childhood when sweets really were special. She finds it hard to accept that what is a treat to her is more like poison to some parents.

"Of all the ways of spoiling grandchildren, I have the biggest problem with food," said one frustrated mother. "Because all those sweets are so unhealthy – and fattening."

Even that most saintly of grandmothers, Jill in Radio 4's *The Archers*, is guilty. In one episode baby Rosie becomes overweight because Jill has been feeding her so many cakes.

"My grandma, who was as round as she was tall, would often bring me treats – a bar of Cadbury's Dairy Milk with fruit and nuts, or maybe a Flake," says Jenni Murray, whose book *Fat Cow* chronicles her lifelong struggle with her weight. "On the rare occasions she had no treats, I'd be given sixpence and allowed to 'pop down the road' to the shop to fill a bag with toffees, Flying Saucers and Sherbet Dip Dabs. I've concluded it's best not to refer to cake, biscuits, sweets and chocolates as treats. The word makes them too desirable – naughty but nice. They're just food!"

Health-conscious parents will refuse to allow their children sweets and chocolates for as long as possible, aware of the dangers of unnecessary sugar. But their rules are often ignored by grannies who persist in indulging the children with forbidden delights, assuming that just a little treat now and then can't do any harm.

The trouble is that babies are generally born liking the sweet taste that they first encounter in their mother's milk. So the earlier you introduce added sugars, the more likely your baby or toddler is to prefer and choose sweet foods into childhood and for the rest of their life. Eating foods that are high in sugar throughout childhood can lead to preventable diseases, such as diabetes, heart disease, obesity, tooth decay and high blood pressure.

Of course the odd lapse is unlikely to do any lasting harm to the child – but it may well affect your relationship with the parents. When you ignore their wishes, you're defying their authority and possibly even losing their trust. So instead of Mars Bars, candy floss, fizzy drinks and bags of Haribou, try instead alternatives that are both wholesome and tasty. It's fine to offer fruit, as it contains less damaging sugar. You could always make your own treats – anything from mashed vegetables with hummous to more ambitious delicacies like pumpkin pancakes, blueberry waffles or banana oat pikelets.

These days, too, there's a huge variety of commercially available titbits for babies. Sainsbury's sells variety packs of organic snacks, for example. Ella's Kitchen offers temptations like spinach bites, vanilla and banana biscuits, sweetcorn and carrot melty sticks, while from Organix you could try cheese crackers for toddlers, or raspberry and apple oat bars.

Grandmothers often joke that their job is to spoil the grandchildren and then send them home. But it's not much fun for the parents to be handed back a screaming toddler high on sugar, or a sulking, sleep-deprived monster. "My husband's mother regarded feeding our three boys as a sacred ritual," Carol told me. "Sunday lunch would be a huge roast with all the trimmings. Then just a couple of hours later she'd provide a full afternoon tea, followed by chocolate. They'd be stuffed to the gills and the eldest, John, would invariably be sick in the car on the way home. It was always at the same point. So when we were approaching Watford Gap we knew to get him out on to the nearest patch of grass."

Food is just one aspect of the perennial conflict between grandparents and parents. Parents who have established firm guidelines for their children are irritated when indulgent grannies allow them to break the rules. They may let them go to bed later, play with forbidden iPads, or – worst of all – they just never say no. When that happens, according to one mum, "they need reprogramming when they get home, having entirely forgotten all their manners."

"Conflict is often generated by grandparents who refuse to uphold the parents' standards for behaviour," according to Susan Adcock, who has written extensively about grandparenting. "This conduct is unacceptable, especially if the grandparents instruct the grandchildren not to tell their parents. This type of behaviour makes cute memes: 'Grandma's House, Grandma's Rules!' 'What Happens at Grandma's Stays at Grandma's!' But in reality, this practice is distinctly unfunny. Such behaviour goes far beyond 'spoiling'. It is instead teaching the grandchildren deceitfulness and lack of respect for the parents.

"Occasionally grandparents don't intend to break the parents' rules but are unsuccessful in getting the children to cooperate. For example, the parent says to put the grandchild to bed at eight, but the grandchild resists falling asleep, and the grandparent is unable to make it happen. In such cases, the grandparents get an A for effort, even if they are not wholly successful."

Another fraught area is present-giving. We all enjoy shopping and giving things to the grandchildren, but parents aren't always happy if we go overboard. For one thing, they may not have room for shedloads of toys. And they worry that the children might start to expect presents with every visit.

"I go abroad a lot for work," Samira said. "And it's so tempting to bring something special each time. But I've stopped doing that now as I don't want them to take it for granted that Granny will always have a present. I was worried that they might look forward to seeing the new toy rather than me."

"We told the grandparents that we were restricting Christmas gifts to four items and we asked them to cut back as well," reported one angry Mumsnet mum. "My mother-in-law showed up with seven gifts."

Harriet's mother-in-law always buys her girls toys and clothes that they don't need, while her own mother just adds money to their savings accounts. "It's so much more appreciated," Harriet said. "They'll really value her contribution as they grow up, and they'll always remember it." But she doesn't like to suggest this to her mother-in-law, who may not be able to afford to give cash.

"What I found most upsetting," Jane confided, "was when the children started saying they didn't love my mum as much as the other granny 'because she doesn't bring me so many presents.'"

Difference in income can create a tension, as the less wealthy grandparents may be concerned that they cannot provide for their grandkids in the same way as their well-off counterparts. Indeed, many grandmas confess they feel threatened by the "other" grandma and so will vie with her for the grandchildren's affection. They may deal with their jealousy by showering the children with ever more presents. Sadly, this competition between the two (or more!) sets of grandparents is quite common – especially between grandmothers.

"My mother-in-law loves to spoil them, but it's become excessive," one desperate mother wrote to Mumsnet. "When she arrives she brings gifts. Every. Bloody. Time. Sometimes it's a small gift (magazine or sweets), other times it's a large toy or money. But always something."

She did try to reason with her mother-in-law. "I asked her to not just hand the gifts straight to the kids, and to ask us first if it's OK. That fell on deaf ears, because the next time she came round with an armful of toys and walked straight in with them." This prompted a furious response. "I actually think she is being hugely disrespectful. I would sit down and explain very clearly one more time and if she does it again I would say, 'I'm sorry, if you are going to continuously undermine our parenting we won't be bringing the kids to you again.'"

"Tell her in no uncertain terms that you're not putting up with this anymore," suggested another mother. "Be prepared for tantrums, but just keep repeating the line 'you know we don't want you to buy the kids stuff, so you can come without it, or you can go home.'"

Not everyone agreed. "Grandparents aren't meant to be parents," wrote one mum. "I think it's nice when a granny spoils a child and treats them to things they aren't usually allowed." "Things don't spoil children," another pointed out. "It's the attitude towards things that makes them spoilt."

Last summer I joined a group of young mothers in the park, where several grannies were happily leading toddlers towards the ice-cream van. I asked them if they minded.

"Of course not," they chorused. "Grannies are supposed to spoil. It's one of the joys."

"He's not allowed any sugar at home, but I don't mind if my mum gives him sweets sometimes," Jane added. "It's no big deal – after all, she doesn't see him that often and it does make them both happy."

But for many families, grandparents' rivalries can be upsetting and divisive.

"Grandparents competing with other grandparents is a sign of insecurity," says marriage and family therapist and grandmother Marilyn Barnicke Belleghem. "By the time adults are old enough to be grandparents, hopefully, they will have learned to be their own personal best and know that competing with others is best left for games."

So what strategies might help you to manage granny rivalry, and to navigate the fine boundary between loving indulgence and harmful spoiling?

Everyone I spoke to agreed that the best solution is, quite simply, to talk. It can be very hurtful to have your gifts rejected, or to be told that your behaviour is bad for your adored grandchild. But even the most stubborn spoiling granny will benefit from listening to what the parents have to say, and will respect them when they explain their own parenting rules.

First of all, get to know the in-laws. At first, the grandparents may not know one another. Why not invite them to spend time together? Building a relationship between them may well ease any feelings of threat or competitiveness.

Do be aware of the circumstances of the other family. If you are better off than they are it's probably not wise to buy expensive presents that they couldn't afford, however tempted you may be by a Ninja ride-on car or a leather rocking-horse. You might end up discovering that those expensive presents are not really welcomed by the children's parents. Many would prefer to cut down waste and avoid cluttering up the planet – or their own tiny flat – by simply hiring toys from rental companies like Whirli Kids Toy Box and giving them back as the child outgrows them. Or you could agree to a shared spending limit, or maybe to replace presents with financial contributions. You may find you have a new friend, with a very precious shared interest.

Remember that love can't be bought. If you want to build a good relationship with your grandchildren, find ways to develop closeness with the children: Skype calls, playing online games together, being Snapchat friends, keeping memory albums, sharing a hobby.

One brilliant way to connect with your grandchildren is to entertain them with your own memories. For centuries grandmothers have taken on the role of Mother Goose, the storyteller who keeps alive traditional tales, songs and rhymes by passing them down through the generations. That function is just as important today, despite the prevalence of CBBC, Disney+ and so many fabulous storybooks.

I don't need to tell you that every baby will clap along to "The Wheels on the Bus", to the point of tedium. But try introducing your grandchild instead to the songs of your own childhood. I've hypnotised quite a few baby relatives with "The Ugly Duckling" or a gutsy rendition of "I Know an Old Lady Who Swallowed a Fly" – complete with the relevant noises. At the right moment, no diversion can enchant a child quite as much as listening to Granny. Grandmothers are natural archivists, preserving family history with accounts of all the ancestors.

My sister's house is crowded with photographs dating back over a hundred years. Her grandson Wolf loves going through all those stern-looking figures, stiffly upright in yellowing sepia, and getting her to identify them. He especially likes to see pictures of his grandfather as a little boy, and to hear about all of his naughty escapades with his crowd of cousins.

Children love to hear stories of your own life.

"My grandma Anne was a powerhouse of a woman," said Cat. "I was extremely close to her, and although she has now passed away I still think about her a lot. She told me loads of stories about her life. She was an RAF engineer in the war – I still have her wings badge. And after my grandfather died she took over his business as leader of a shipping and fine art business. She was a formidable woman who wouldn't take any bullshit and always spoke her mind. She loved people and was still making new friends well into her 90s! She once told a bloke at the theatre to fuck off, really loudly, and she would flirt with every single waiter whenever we went out for a meal. Anne never lost her spirit, even when she finally began to get frail. 'I've lived a strong life, and now I'm going to have a strong death,' she announced. She'd always been a great partygoer. Her final words were so fitting. 'I want to go to the party on the cruise ship.'"

Four-year-old Sebastian was so fascinated by the tales of his Caribbean grandmother that he recorded an interview with her, in which she described how she came to the UK with *Windrush* and, despite the difficulties she faced, worked her way up from cleaning lady to senior nurse in charge of a ward in an NHS hospital.

My daughter used to be entranced by her centenarian granny's memories. As a little girl in the First World War she used to be sent to the market for oyster shells to feed to the chickens (to strengthen the shells of their eggs); later she was a "Nippy" (waitress) in a Lyons teashop, and once served tea to Virginia Woolf. Then there were her Second World War stories: trying to cross London with three children during the Blitz, only to be rescued from the falling bombs by a friendly bus conductor; queuing for precious sweets because of rationing; drawing lines on the backs of her legs because she couldn't get hold of stockings.

"Remember that your grandchildren will probably forget expensive presents and trips," advises Rob Parsons, author of *The Sixty Minute Grandparent*. "But they will look back and remember the times of fun and the feeling that you made them feel special."

"The best grandmas don't give a toy and watch the grandchildren play," Susan Adcock advises. "They play with the grandchildren. They give their undivided attention and unconditional love. That's one type of spoiling that no one can object to."

Sometimes, though, the relationship can be soured by quite different kinds of rivalry: between the grandmother and her daughter-in-law. "It's safe to say that the thought of 'your mother-in-law being jealous of you' has at least crossed your mind once," according to an article in the *Ghana Guardian*. "After all, every mother-in-law feels a little bit jealous when their little boys grow up to be men and marry the girl of their dreams. Surely, mothers feel happy about their sons but get jealous when they tend to put their wives as the first priority. This can get really frustrating for the daughter-in-law."

The journalist then quoted some mothers-in-law who confess to resenting their sons' wives. "To be honest, I have always been a little possessive," admitted one. "So when I finally got to know that my son was intending to get married, I knew I had to be ready to face whoever it is. My daughter-in-law is very sweet and kind, and I'm grateful that she is there for my son. But I couldn't help but think of the fact that now, there's another precious woman in his life."

Another jealous woman was even more outraged. "My daughter-in-law has the audacity to turn my son against me! My son is so innocent that he can't understand that woman's behaviour at all. Instead, he takes her side and tells me off for being very rude!"

According to a study of hundreds of families over two decades, more than 60 per cent of women admitted the relationship with their female in-law caused them long-term unhappiness and stress.

Dr Terri Apter, in carrying out the research for her book *What Do You Want From Me?*, found that two-thirds of daughters-in-law believed that their husband's mother frequently exhibited jealous maternal love towards their sons: making demands, being critical or intrusive, sulking and eliciting pity.

A similar proportion of mothers-in-law, however, complained of being excluded and isolated. One heartbroken mother offered me a whole set of baby clothes when my granddaughter was born. "I'd saved them for when my son and daughter-in law came to visit," she explained. "But they still haven't, and I know it's because she just doesn't like me."

When Yvonne was seriously ill in hospital she was surprised by a visit from her grown-up granddaughter, whom she hadn't seen for years. "How much has your mum told you about me?" she asked. The answer was that the young woman had grown up knowing nothing about her grandmother at all. It was as if the daughter-in-law seemed to have tried to obliterate her.

Apter, who spent 20 years interviewing hundreds of families across the world, found that the in-law problem is almost always between the two women. "As they struggle to achieve the same position in the family as primary woman," she said, "each tries to establish or protect her status, each feels threatened by the other."

Quite often loving mothers may not even be aware of their jealousy of the woman who has usurped them. So do reflect on how you respond to and treat your daughter-in-law.

"By taking steps to work through difficult feelings and release any resentment you may feel, you can reduce the likelihood that you respond or speak in a way that is damaging to the relationship," advises Susan Adcock. "It's vital that you not only embrace your new role, but that you also develop a respectful, empathetic, and encouraging relationship with your adult child's partner."

Of course, that applies to your son and daughter-in-law too, as this furious ex-wife reported to the website Quora. "My ex-mother-in-law always insulted me. She never was nice and when I called she'd ask who was calling. When I'd say, 'Susan', she'd say, 'Susan who?' Only one Susan in the family. She'd come to visit and spend hours telling my husband how unhappy she was with me. She'd tell my children how mean I was to her (not true). My husband never defended me. One day after 10 years of this crap, my ex said, 'Mama can say and do anything she wants.' I told him if he wouldn't defend me he could go live with his beloved 'mama'. He, of course, didn't want to do that. I reminded him that when he married me he was supposed to orient to me and not to his mother. He didn't want to do that. So, I filed for divorce."

Another Quora contributor was more understanding. "Let's face it: the daughter-in-law is removing her son," wrote Eloise. "That saying, 'A son's a son till he takes a wife, but a daughter's a daughter all her life', is true. Don't know why, but it is. But a mother-in-law who blames her daughter-in-law for it is being silly, self-centered, and selfish. She should be friends with the girl if she has any sense. That's not to say the son may not have married the ideal mate, and the girl could be a perfect idiot, but the mother who's losing a son should be as perfect and gracious as she's ever been in her life."

If family rifts are not repaired, everyone will be affected. The children may miss out on a warm, untroubled relationship with their grandma, and your son will be uncomfortable with the coolness between the two women he loves most. But you will suffer the most, if you miss all the grandchildren's milestones or, even worse, find yourself completely estranged from them. So it's up to you to make sure that doesn't happen, and to do all you can to get along with your daughter-in-law. To begin with, the best way to build a sense of trust is to be respectful of the couple's time and relationship. That means you need to avoid being critical.

"Right from when we got married my mother-in-law made it clear that I wasn't up to her exacting standards," confided Sasha. "She just couldn't let go of her darling son. She even used to come round each morning to lay out his shirt and make sure he had matching socks. That was annoying enough. But it was even more extreme once the children came along. She'd try to mother them as well. Eventually we moved further away and that seemed to work."

Sometimes unsolicited help can be seen as an outright attack. Even your attempts to be useful can be interpreted as thinly veiled criticisms. You may, for example, think you're being kind and helpful if you clean the parents' house without being asked. But instead, it may look as if you believe they are bad housekeepers.

So don't barge in with mop and cleaning fluids, with a plan to attack the neglected bathroom. Try not to tut with disapproval if the kitchen is piled with dirty dishes; don't run your finger meaningfully along dusty surfaces; leave the fridge alone even if you're itching to throw away mouldy cheese and ready meals that are weeks past their sell-by date. Don't turn up your nose at those ready meals, either. For a busy new mum they could be a life-saver.

Instead, just ask how you can help: offer to cook dinner, get the shopping, change the nappy or watch the baby for a while to give the exhausted mother a break.

Your eagerness to help may be well-meant, but don't overdo it: don't arrive at every visit with a home-cooked meal, or a fridgeful of groceries. Even if they are grateful at first, the couple may well start to resent your generosity as interference. Make sure you respect their privacy. Don't drop by without calling, for example, even if you have an emergency key. They'll appreciate it if you call first and ask to pop in – and don't be offended if they say it's not convenient.

"Remember that you're not the child's mother," warns Adcock. "Your role as a grandmother is different – and, some would say, even better. So don't try to take on responsibilities that don't belong to you. Instead, leave the parenting to your adult child and their partner and focus instead on loving your grandchildren."

Just be the best mother-in-law you can be: kind, friendly, supportive and respectful. Here's a reminder that when relationships get thorny you must never, ever lose your sense of humour. This story should help:

Sadie and Becky met again after many years and began exchanging histories. "Whatever happened to your son?" asked Sadie.

"Oh, what a tragedy!" moaned Becky. "My son married a no-good who doesn't lift a finger around the house. She can't cook, she can't sew a button on a shirt, all she does is sleep. My poor boy brings her breakfast in bed, and all day long she stays there, loafing, reading, eating chocolates!"

"That's terrible," sympathised Sadie. "And what about your daughter?"

"Oh, she's got a good life. She married a man who's a living doll! He won't let her set foot in the kitchen. He gives her breakfast in bed, and makes her stay there all day, resting, reading, and eating chocolates."

My Grandmother
by Elizabeth Jennings

She kept an antique shop – or it kept her.
Among Apostle spoons and Bristol glass,
The faded silks, the heavy furniture,
She watched her own reflection in the brass
Salvers and silver bowls, as if to prove
Polish was all, there was no need of love.

And I remember how I once refused
To go out with her, since I was afraid.
It was perhaps a wish not to be used
Like antique objects. Though she never said
That she was hurt, I still could feel the guilt
Of that refusal, guessing how she felt.

Later, too frail to keep a shop, she put
All her best things in one long narrow room.
The place smelt old, of things too long kept shut.
The smell of absences where shadows come
That can't be polished. There was nothing then
To give her own reflection back again.

And when she died I felt no grief at all,
Only the guilt of what I once refused.
I walked into her room among the tall
Sideboards and cupboards – things she never used
But needed: and no finger-marks were there,
Only the new dust falling through the air.

Five

Mind That Child!

When Joanne told her friend Patsy that her daughter was pregnant she was taken aback by her response. "Great! You're going to be a grandmother!" exclaimed Patsy. "So you'd better give in your notice now. You won't have time to work once the baby's arrived."

Joanne was aghast. It had never crossed her mind that being a grandmother would be a full-time job. In fact, she hadn't considered it a job at all. But then she realised that Patsy had meant well. She'd assumed that all grandmothers would be as hands-on as she was, with her three delightful charges taking up not just most of her time but a big chunk of her waking thoughts as well. She picks up the two older ones from school most days, looks after the baby three times a week, and often has all of them to stay.

Patsy is not alone. According to a 2017 survey by the charity Age UK, almost two in ten of the nation's grandparents aged over 50 provide regular childcare for their children's children. That's around five million grandparents. Of these,

89 per cent provide childcare for their grandchildren at least once a week, while 12 per cent do so every day. Since that survey was published, the number is likely to have increased, given the staggering costs of nurseries and childminders.

For many parents the cost of childcare care has been so enormous that mothers have had to stay at home. Brandishing slogans like "Women should not have to pay to work," "The future won't raise itself" and "My skills got me hired! My work got me fired!" thousands of women took part in 2022 in The March of the Mummies, a furious protest organised by the pressure group Pregnant then Screwed against the crippling costs of childcare.

Back then, the subsidy of 15 hours a week only applied to three- and four-year olds. Full-time nursery for children under the age of two cost almost two-thirds of a parent's weekly take-home pay. As a result of a reduction in the number of nurseries and childminders, many mothers – 87,000, according to the Office for National Statistics – were unable to work as they either couldn't find or couldn't afford childcare.

Back then, the subsidy of 15 hours a week only applied to three- and four-year olds. Full-time nursery for children under the age of two cost almost two-thirds of a parent's weekly take-home pay. As a result of a reduction in the number of nurseries and childminders, many mothers – 87,000, according to the Office for National Statistics – were unable to work as they either couldn't find or couldn't afford childcare.

In 2024 the government introduced a more generous policy, to be phased in over two years. The 15 hours of free childcare were extended to all children from the age of nine months. From September 2025 working parents of children under the age of five would become entitled to 30 hours of free childcare per week, while some with greater needs would be entitled to more. The changes are intended to help mothers to go back to work and bolster our faltering economy – since they and the nursery workers would all pay tax.

But since it was announced, the policy has attracted the fury of nurseries. Many face closure as they struggle to balance their books, with insufficient funding and difficulties retaining staff. The problem, according to nurseries, is that the hourly rate set by government for free places doesn't meet the cost. So the number of nurseries closing is a major concern. Numbers of early year providers dropped dramatically even before the new policy was announced.

Since then, parents have been finding it increasingly difficult to secure places for their children, so while they welcome the new financial support, many have continued to struggle. "We're hearing all the time that costs are increasing outside the funded hours and parents are seeing very large increases in the cost of consumables like food and nappies as nurseries look to make up shortfall," said Joeli Brearley, CEO of campaign group Pregnant Then Screwed. "The overall savings are far less than families had anticipated."

Under the new arrangements, the government has also raised the required staff ratio in nurseries from 1:4 to 1:5, while childminders are allowed to take up to six children per person. These ratios have always been contentious. Boris Johnson launched a consultation on a similar plan for nurseries. Then Liz Truss considered scrapping the whole idea of caps. Reduced ratios, it was claimed, would mean fewer staff so nurseries could reduce their fees.

But both staff and parents are against any such reduction in the ratios. Indeed, last time Truss suggested such a reduction, in 2013, more than 20,000 parents signed a petition opposing it. What's more, there's no guarantee that nurseries would pass on these savings to their clients.

So it's not surprising that many parents are turning to their own parents for help. When they do, the primary caregiver is increasingly likely to be the grandmother. So now may be a good time for you to consider just how much time you're going to devote to seeing and looking after your grandchild. There are so many reasons why spending quality time with him or her will be good for everyone: the child, the parents and you yourself.

You'll benefit from the close bond that will develop right from the start. The child will have an extra adoring, trustworthy adult in her life. You can never have too many of those. With you to rely on, the parents can enjoy a much-needed babysitting break in the early months. Later on, they'll so appreciate your willingness to fill in when needed, whether it's to pick up from school, step in when the child is ill, or take the child or children on treats and outings.

You're more likely to have more time than the parents, especially if you've retired. Even then, of course, you're bound to live a busy, active life. But you'll be more flexible, more able to provide help when needed. As well as the real enjoyment of being with young children, you'll also benefit from the stimulation and exercise that looking after them involves.

It's commonly believed that looking after grandchildren makes you feel younger and more energetic. But that's a bit of a myth, according to a 2016 study, *Is There a Rejuvenating*

Effect of (Grand)Childcare? The authors, Valeria Bordone and Bruno Arpino, interviewed grandparent carers before and after their responsibilities began, and found that their duties hadn't made much difference to their health. It's really, they argued, that those who are fitter in the first place are more likely to take on childcare responsibilities. "It may well be that personality traits and family values that mean grandparents already have a young, subjective age are overrepresented among individuals who provide care to others," they said.

One surprising result of the research was the discovery that there are slight benefits in older adults looking after young children who are not their own kin. Bordone suggested that unrelated children bring with them the rejuvenating effect of youth – without the reminder of old age that comes with grandchildren.

So it may be a relief not to feel guilty if you can't always drop everything to help out with the grandchildren. But how often should you see them? As often as possible, asserted Vanessa Feltz, who in 2015 was voted Celebrity Grandmother of the Year in a poll conducted by the restaurant chain Table Table. Vanessa, who has three grandchildren, sees them every day if she can, and takes time off in the school holidays to look after them. She was shocked by the results of a World Jewish Relief survey that showed that one-third of adult Jews see their grandparents only four times a year or less. She urged young people to "buck up their ideas and go and see their grandparents immediately."

"When I was growing up," she said, "we saw my grandparents at least once a week. I would go to Grandma Zibbles on Friday night for dinner and Grandma Babs on Sunday. I adored them. I don't even think once a week is enough."

But if you can't visit your own granny, how about finding a new one? That's what Max Wallis did. "My gran died last year and I miss her a lot," he wrote in *The Guardian* in May 2024. "But now I'm finding solace in the TikTok accounts of other older people." Max developed a close bond with 89-year-old Norma. "She has a deep commitment to Morrisons fish and chips, lovers butter mints, and is always trying to slip her granddaughter a tenner. That's what Norma is like. It feels as though we've grown close in recent weeks. But the truth is, I've never met her. I'm one of her 2 million followers on TikTok, checking in daily to see what she has been up to."

Max is not the only one. He reported that "a recent poll found that 66% of gen Z and millennials enjoy watching videos featuring older people; 78% say they learned a lot from them." Nan Tok, he added, is now a global phenomenon. "Gangsta Granny lives in Ohio and is a veritable pensioner A-lister, with 396m likes on TikTok. In Taiwan, octogenarian launderette owner Hsu Sho-Er and her husband, Chang Wan-Ji, showcased fashion 'lewks' made from customers' abandoned clothing on their Instagram account. When Hsu Sho-Er died in May last year, their 727,000 followers mourned. Such is the ingrained community of NanTok."

But children shouldn't be forced to see their grandparents at all, according to the Italian supreme court. In 2023, after a protracted battle in Milan when grandparents were pitted against parents in claiming their rights, the court finally ruled that visits should be up to the children themselves.

Vanessa would no doubt be incredulous at such a draconian measure – and she wouldn't be alone. Quite a few of the feminist baby boomers I've spoken to seem to be just as passionate about taking on the task of being what

Vanessa called "the best grandma in the history of grandma-hood". I wonder whether some at least may be unconsciously making up for when, as young mothers desperately juggling demanding jobs and family, they didn't spend as much time with their children as they would have liked.

Jasmine, for example, a highly respected museum administrator tipped for a major promotion, jacked in her job when her first grandchild arrived. Phoebe, who used to pride herself on managing a huge IT business while relying on an army of nannies and au pairs to cope with her four children, now takes over her grandchildren at least twice a week and for quite a few weekends.

My feminist friends roundly dismiss the idea that they should feel guilty about their choices. "I do have more time to spend with them, now that I'm no longer working," Tess said. "But that doesn't mean I neglected my own children when I was a working mum. I always put them first."

Anna agreed. "I think the secret is to be relaxed with whatever arrangements you've made. I went back to work very soon after my daughter was born, and she's turned out fine. I hate the assumption that because we were working we were somehow bad mothers."

They all love the freedom they now have to be brilliant grandmothers. Gransnet has found that 51 per cent of grandparents regularly look after their grandchildren all year round, Most often they're looking after two grandchildren for one or two days a week (56 per cent of grandcarers), although a minority (7 per cent) provide childcare five days a week. A further 10 per cent say they help out during school holidays.

Gransnet reported that while one in six grandparents have taken early retirement or quit paid employment to help out with their grandchildren, 80 per cent of them say their sacrifice is worth it, and more than half (51 per cent) say they're happier now they spend time with their grandchildren.

"I just love being with them," said Carolyn, "especially now that my granddaughters are older. It's lovely to do things with them, to find out what they're up to at school, to play with them and really talk about things."

But such intensive grandmothering isn't for everyone. Prue Leith, who has ten grandchildren, tends to keep her distance, even though she adores them. "Oh, I'm a rotten grandmother – there's no question about it!" she confessed cheerfully to *Good Housekeeping*. "Every time I see them I think, 'I missed that bit,' because they've grown another six inches."

Diane is similarly unrepentant. "Of course I see my grandchildren regularly," she said. "About once a month. It's more than enough."

An article in *The Times* in 2023 described some of the tensions that arise when grandparents take on regular childcare. Lucia and Chris, both in their 70s, are part of a growing army of grandparents who, through necessity as much as desire, are ever more involved in caring for their grandchildren. "We are a tireless, unpaid army and the government are very lucky to have us," Lucia said.

Geraldine Bedell told *The Times* that she resents the moral pressure placed on grandparents to provide care. "My children have friends whose parents travel miles to look after their grandchildren, putting in long hours on their hands and knees with building blocks and Lego. These people are saints. I do not do this. They make me feel inadequate.

"I know, as the founding editor of Gransnet, that for every grandparent who's happy to shoulder the responsibility of childcare, there are others who feel put upon. Or, if they resist the (undoubted) need for their help, who feel guilty."

The Times also pointed out that the Gransnet and Mumsnet online forums teem with grandmothers tired of entitled offspring expecting childcare on tap, and exhausted parents aggrieved that their own parents or in-laws aren't offering more help. "We often have to reschedule work commitments to fit in with grandkids' needs, and cancel social invitations," wrote one disgruntled granny who looks after her grandchildren up to five times a week. "We adore our grandchildren and love being involved in their lives," she added, but "my daughter and her husband don't often show appreciation."

Gransnet editor Lara Crisp pointed out that some are occasionally left feeling that too much is expected of them and that they are taken for granted, while others have even reported falling out with their children when requests for childcare are not met. "It's important to be up front from the start about what you can and can't handle, but remember – although you love your grandchildren, they are not your responsibility."

"My mum has never looked after my children," wrote one Mumsnet contributor. "She made it clear it wasn't happening and it was 'my choice to have them'. I actually prefer knowing it's not really her thing, it is after all her time to do what she wants now her own children have grown up!"

"I have never asked for or expected any childcare from my parents or my in-laws," another mother agreed. "My children have brilliant relationships with all their grandparents and they all love one another very much. It is lovely when grandparents feel able to help with childcare and certainly helps financially but I don't think it should be expected."

Many of us would sympathise with her. Looking after children can be exhausting however fit you may be. So it's important to be honest with yourself as well as with your son or daughter about how much you can manage. Babysitting occasionally, picking up from school, having the children over for the day sometimes – all of these are what most of us would expect to do and to thoroughly enjoy. But how about taking on the full role of childminder – every day?

For some families this can be a great solution, and the arrangement can work really well, according to some of the respondents to a 2020 survey by BabyCentre.

"My parents are great and follow my rules. They look after my son while I'm at work and are always accommodating if I'm running late."

"My mum and my wife's mum take turns looking after my son. It works out really well! They're happy to cook for him, and even take him to toddler groups. Obviously we pay for days out and food, but it's still so much cheaper than other childcare options."

Others, though, pointed out some of the drawbacks. Obviously, it's important that you have a good understanding in the first place, so it's important to discuss the ground rules before you start.

One mother offered her own solution. "My mother-in-law looks after our daughter. In the run-up, we invited her over as much as possible so she could get a sense of our parenting style. It also meant that we could discuss any potential issues well in advance. It made for a really smooth transition."

"My mother is an absolute star and nightmare rolled into one," explained one frustrated mother. "She gives in to all my daughter's demands. I then have to deal with tantrums and my toddler saying, 'Nanny lets me do it!' I've explained how difficult this makes things for me, and my mum is finally getting the message!"

One way to avoid undiscussed problems becoming serious issues may be to draw up a Family Childcare Agreement in order to provide clarity about childcare arrangements. This might include specifying the hours and days, the location, and even details like behaviour and discipline management, suitable foods, and safety issues, especially if you'll be looking after the children at home.

While many grandparents would welcome the opportunity for discussion, others might balk at such formality. After all, it's your own child, your own grandchild you're dealing with. Maybe you'd be happier with just a handwritten reminder of some of the basic details, or even a note on the fridge.

Some grannies, on the other hand, don't agree that there should be any agreement at all – like this contributor to Gransnet, who is adamant that grandparents are under no obligation to take care of grandchildren. "You cannot get on with your life with babies in tow, you cannot lunch with your friends, play golf, relax at the spa, walk over the hills, even browse the shops with small people. If you have to give up what you had planned for your retirement because your grandchildren are constantly hanging onto your skirts, you deserve to be fully financially compensated."

So how would you feel about charging for looking after the children?

That was part of Liz Truss's plan during her short-lived regime. Her proposal was to alter the childcare subsidy so that parents, rather than nurseries, be given government cash to spend as they see fit. That would mean the cash could be passed on to grandparents to take on the job.

But not everyone would be happy accepting hard cash. Most of the grandmothers I've spoken to are horrified at the idea. "I can't see that any grandparent would happily accept money for looking after their own grandchildren," one incredulous mother said. "I'm more than happy to help out – and I enjoy being with the children."

Once the arrangement becomes financial there's so much potential for conflict. How much to pay? How many hours? Contributors to Gransnet have even reported falling out with their children when requests for childcare are not met.

Busy grandmothers may resent being relegated to the role of nanny-in-chief, once again having their independence curtailed by all the paraphernalia of childcare: nappy-changing, afternoon sleeps, the constant demands of tantrummy toddlers, their endless questions, refusals to eat or put on their shoes, that ominous crunch of plastic underfoot.

Another mother stressed how important it is to offer a quality experience for the child. "I have no say in what my mum feeds him or where she takes him, that's her decision, and if they stayed in then so be it (she rarely does) but if you're paying they should at least spend that money on doing things with him."

In any case, grandparents may not always be the ideal carers. We've seen how some of them may spoil the children. Also, for every grandparent who'll happily take them to the park, cook with them, visit museums, play Poo Bingo and talk to them, there are many others who will plonk the children in front of the television, or allow them to play with laptops without even supervising what they're browsing.

Grandparents, after all, won't have had any formal training in the role. They may not be aware, for example, how important it is for toddlers to be with other children in the early years. According to research by the Institute of Education, small children who go to nursery are much better prepared for school than those who are looked after by their grandparents.

Some grannies may not expect to be paid but most would appreciate some form of thanks, even if it was just the occasional present or treat. As ever, the best way to smooth out any potential problems is to discuss what is expected of you, and how much you regard as reasonable. If parents are able to pay you for childcare, they might welcome the arrangement just as much as you. "When I want things done a certain way, my mum often has other ideas," one mother wrote to Mumsnet. "But because I'm paying her, she'll do it my way regardless. Making the arrangement a bit more formal has probably saved us a few arguments!"

So how much is a reasonable amount to pay? This can vary enormously, according to just how much is involved and for how long. Back in 2022 one mother said she pays the grandparents £250 a month for looking after a toddler and a school-age child all day. Another gives her mother just £120 for just one toddler, but adds petrol money, and pays for the nappies and food. For many families these rates have increased each year. Even then, the cost is a great deal more manageable than nursery fees. But for some grandparents it's simply not acceptable.

Gloria, who is from the Philippines, works five days a week as a cleaner. But she still picks up her two grandchildren every afternoon and looks after them until her daughter picks them up at bedtime – and sometimes not even then. "My daughter and her husband both work so hard, and the least I can do is give them a break for a couple of hours. I wouldn't dream of accepting any money." In her country, she explained, it's natural for grandparents to step in to help. There would never be any question of payment. This view is shared in many countries across the world.

In China, for example, it's common for older Chinese people to take an active role in raising the grandchildren, in order to help them with their education and future careers. Like Ida Lang, for example, in Hong Kong. Her daily routine is described by Kelly Yang, in *The Atlantic* magazine.

"68-year-old Ida Lang wakes up every morning at six. Like most retirees, she loves the calm of the morning, which she has all to herself. But unlike other retirees, Ida's me-time lasts for exactly one hour. At seven, she goes to her younger son's house, where for the next eight hours, Ida feeds, plays with, changes and talks to her son's newborn daughter. Then at three, she's off to her other shift, this time at her older son's house. There, she supervises homework, teaches, plays make-believe games and reads to her eight-year-old granddaughter and four-year-old grandson until well past nine, when their parents get home."

She's not unusual. In most traditional cultures grandmothers are accorded immense dignity and respect. They are considered powerful matriarchs, fountains of wisdom who are trusted to pass on cultural rituals and beliefs. Some will have religious functions, too. In many

South African villages the chief grandmother tends the sacred fire which must be kept burning at all times, and will light any new ceremonial fire.

Rather gloriously, when a Japanese grandmother turns 61 there's a party to celebrate her arrival at the final stage of her life. From then on she must be treated with great consideration, her wishes granted, her opinions valued. Old age is not a disability a person tries to ignore but a triumph.

In pre-industrial communities birth is considered a matter for the whole family, usually with the grandmother as the linchpin. Among many South African tribes a woman will go back to her grandmother's home to give birth, while both grandmother and mother will attend the birth. On the islands of Fiji not only will the woman's mother be present at the birth, she will also supervise the pregnancy. It is considered shameful if a woman delivers the baby without the women of the family being there for her. In Korea it's the mother-in-law who is responsible for preparing her son's wife for the birth and for supporting her through labour.

Evolutionary biologists and anthropologists have long wondered why women, unlike other animals, continue to live after the menopause, once their own reproductive years are over. So they have come up with "the grandmother hypothesis" – the idea that grandmothers like Ida are crucial for the health and even the survival of the next generation.

Kristen Hawkes, a professor of anthropology at the University of Utah, has extensively studied the Hadza, a group of hunter-gatherers in Tanzania who eat a lot of wild foods such as berries and tubers. While young children can pick berries themselves, older women in the community are the ones pulling up the more unyielding bulbous root vegetables, which would be difficult for young kids. Hawkes found that grandmothers who stepped in to help with the work and, especially, with the children allowed the mothers to concentrate on having more children. She and like-minded collaborators argued that grandmothers are a driving force behind the increased longevity of our species compared to other primates. In other words, they aimed to prove the validity of "the grandmother hypothesis".

In Malawi, grandparents are shown great respect in their community and regarded as a source of information, wisdom and comfort. But healthcare workers there were concerned about the levels of illiteracy, which meant that not everyone was familiar with modern practices. So the Alangizi Association developed programmes to update the skills of grandmothers, with very positive results. They found that these grandmothers were open to new ideas and were able to combine their traditional knowledge of matters like nutrition and reproductive health with up-to-date advice.

It's not just in that community that grandparents can benefit from advice and support. We're all aware of how much has changed since we had children ourselves, and may be wary about the validity of our own knowledge. But what hasn't changed is the huge importance of grandparents, everywhere: our ability to offer comfort and confidence, the wisdom of our experience and our willingness to help, and to be there for the children and their parents whenever we're needed. That's our great strength. That, and our unremitting fountain of love.

Granny Granny Please Comb My Hair
by Grace Nichols

Granny Granny
Please comb my hair.
You always take your time,
You always take such care.

You put me to sit on a cushion
Between your knees;
You rub a little coconut oil,
Parting gentle as a breeze.

Mummy Mummy
She's always in a hurry-hurry rush
She pulls my hair
Sometimes she tugs.

But Granny
You have all the time in the world,
And when you're finished
You always turn my head and say,
"Now, who's a nice girl?"

Six

Playing Safe

You may visit regularly to look after the baby or to play with your grandchildren. But are you ready to welcome them into your own home?

Remember how, when you had your first baby, the whole world began to seem like one giant, looming threat? It's just as threatening when you're looking after grandchildren. "Oh, it's much worse," says my friend Tess. "I'm constantly looking out for danger. We've moved everything up to top shelves, hidden all the matches, invested in a baby gate. I've plugged in all the electrical sockets and still worry that someone will trip over one of the television cables. I've even occasionally screamed at the toddler when he tries to switch on *Peppa Pig* himself. I've turned into a panicking harridan."

She's not alone. So many of the grandmothers I've spoken to confess that they feel quite nervous when the children come to visit. The streams of advice that are available often seem designed to feed their anxiety.

I mean, obviously it's important to keep the house clean. But how clean?

"As babies and toddlers crawl, sit, lie on the floor or carpet and put toys in their mouth, grandparents should upkeep a clean and healthy environment for their loved ones to explore," warns Daisy Ching from Go Cleaners. "The best results can be achieved by using professional steam or dry cleaning of carpets and furniture with eco-friendly and child-safe detergents."

Fantastic Tradesmen excels in instilling paranoia among even the most safety-conscious granny. "Install soft corner protectors to allow children to walk or run safely around the furniture. Protect children from cabinet corners, beds, tables and so forth. Make sure all cabinets, wardrobes, cupboards and bookcases are thoroughly scrutinised as curious little hands or fingers can get injured if they are thrust in. Install cabinet locks on most handles and knobs. It's always better not to rely solely on safety locks – remove all dangerous objects or put them out of children's reach. Make sure that all wardrobes, bookcases, cabinets and TVs are well stabilised and fit to the wall as they can cause significant injury to the child if they accidentally fall over."

Almost everything is a hazard, warns The Consumer Product Safety Commission (CPSC). "On average one child dies every two weeks as a result of top-heavy furniture falling over," it unhelpfully reminds us. "Unstable chests of drawers are a major culprit, especially when there is a TV on the top. Hang your flat-screen TV or, if that isn't possible, *securely anchor* it to the stand."

Don't forget to childproof the kitchen. "Turn off and store in a safe place all movable appliances when not in use,"

Daisy Ching insists. She almost seems to relish the list of potential dangers. "Kitchen robots, juicers, toasters and etc. If a child can pull or suffer a burn by a hot iron, hair drier, or a domestic heater, then precautions are a must."

You may think the garden is an ideal playground for children, especially if you have room for a paddling pool, a slide, even a sandpit. It's fun to teach them about flowers, encourage them to water the plants, even to have their own plot to tend. But have you considered the menace lurking in the grass?

"Unsecured flower pots can easily tip, fall or even worse, hurt a child," warns Fantastic Tradesmen. "Make sure pots are either out of hands' reach or heavy enough to eliminate such accidents. Look into ways to make the pot base heavier i.e. secure the pots within gabion walls, safety anchors or glue it if you wish to. Another solution is to hang the flower pots as high as possible Soil and plants themselves may be poisonous if swallowed too. Take the time to properly store and secure any gardening tools that might pose the risk of harm, such as lawnmowers, trimmers, especially saws or other blades."

Some advice is even more outlandish. Be careful to hide your guns, urges one American (obviously) site. Keep children away from naked flames, suggests another. Don't let them play with knives.

Most grandparents will keep special toys and activities for when the children visit. But watch out – these can be deadly, according to the CPSC. "If a baby plays with a toy that has small parts or long fur, they might choke or swallow bits of the toy."

And you'd better watch out for magnets – they're a straight route to intensive care. "Swallowing a high-powered magnet set can be fatal to anyone, but this can be particularly hazardous for small children. Even building and play sets with small magnets that are suitable for older children should be off limits to small children, who are inclined to put things in their mouths."

It's not surprising that so many grandmothers have become cautious, as the children's parents today are so bombarded with information and dire warnings. Everything seems so regulated. "How many vegetables did she eat?" my daughter will ask after leaving the toddler with me. "How much screen time did she have? Did she sleep more than 40 minutes?"

The demands of the parents can sap the energy of grandmothers. "I dread the day each week when I care for my grandson," confided one Gransnet contributor. "He is charming and obedient, funny and healthy and perfectly normal but I am exhausted with worry by 7.30pm. What is wrong with me? I had three children of my own and remember days of chaos and tiredness, frustration and laughter but never this level of worry."

So parents' anxieties tend to be passed on to grandparents – usually grandmothers – to the point where sometimes concern about safety can override everything else. According to new research, this could be a reflection of the current trend in intensive parenting.

This approach, which began to be practised in America in the 1990s, is centred solely on the needs of children, encompassing all aspects of emotional, psychological and cognitive development. Benedetta Cappellini, Professor of Marketing at Durham University, is one of the authors of a new study exploring how parenting styles can influence grandparents. "Intensive parenting," she explains, "requires concerted cultivation rather than natural growth. Childrearing is seen as a project with skills to be learnt, targets to be achieved and money to be spent."

Parents become obsessive about school, crowd each day with extra-curricular activities and ensure that every experience is somehow improving, all in the quest for perfection. It's as if the child becomes a proxy of the parents' identity – any success a reflection of their success.

Cappellini found that grandmothers sometimes had mixed feelings about their role as educators, even though they usually followed the parents' wishes as they believed these were "best for the child". They tended to regard activities like homework or attending courses with children as duties and in some cases as a self-sacrifice, reflecting the attitude of those parents who practised intensive parenting.

On the whole, the respondents in the survey were happy with the role of educator, but not so happy with imposing too much discipline, or with the occasional conflicts. So they'd be more likely to do these tasks their own way, and certainly didn't feel as competitive as the parents.

"I do like to help them with homework," one grandmother told me. "But I try to make it fun – getting them to explain things to me, for example, or else creating quizzes or tests with prizes." Another admitted to resorting to a most familiar, time-honoured teaching method. "I bribe them," she said cheerfully. "Special treat if you finish your Maths; choose your own TV show if you get your essay done by dinner time. I'm quite shameless – I'll try anything."

There's so much emphasis on the "right" way to do things, says Cappellini, that grandmothers have to fit into a relentlessly strict regime. That can lead to tension as they try to follow rules they may not agree with. One grandmother was castigated for investing in the "wrong" brand of car seat, even though she could see nothing wrong with it. Others got into trouble for allowing the children to download games on the iPad – sometimes not realising which ones were forbidden.

If the rules are too strict, some reported that they didn't like to feel they had to "report back" to the parents, and some just rebelled, letting them watch *Frozen*, say, or allowing them a wicked slice of cake. One grandmother I spoke to cheerfully admitted that when the children visited she'd definitely ignore her daughter's set of instructions. "In my house it's my rules. But we don't tend to tell the parents…"

Several of the women in Cappellini's study said they resented having to help with homework, or take the children to after-school classes. "I'm just a taxi," one grandmother complained. "If all I'm doing is driving them around then there's no time left just to be together."

In the *Sunday Times* several years ago, Eleanor Mills suggested that some grandmothers are so fed up with the rigid routines required by so many of today's parents that they're tempted to give up looking after the children altogether. "Gen-Xers – the creators of helicopter parenting – are far more intensively involved in stimulating and programming their children's lives than their parents were," she wrote. "A glance at Gransnet shows that even the hands-on grannies chafe at the burdens of 21st-century parenting. As they tussle with car seats (back in the 1970s no one bothered) and get told off for feeding the kids biscuits, or food that isn't organic, it is not surprising some choose to opt out.

"Gransnet is full of older women biting their tongues, sharing their terror that something awful will happen to their grandchildren while they are in their charge (which their ogre offspring would never forgive them for) and reminiscing about how in their day they just chucked the children outside to play."

That is the main reason why so many of the grandmothers in Cappellini's study were resentful. They wanted to have fun with the children, rather than see themselves as protectors or educators. And that's something that the children themselves value most. Nine-year-old Isla told me that her granny does always ask how school is going, and she'll devise spelling quizzes for her and her sister. But best of all are the special times they spend together. "She sometimes takes me to Kew Gardens to teach me about the flowers, and we go swimming. We also play lots of board games. And one time she taught me how to do Sudoku."

Rob, who has two young children of his own, is still very close to his nan. He and his brother loved their time with her when they were growing up. "We used to cook and bake with her," he remembered. "And as she used to be a dress-maker she taught us sewing and how to cut out patterns."

Ruby, six, and her little brother Wren just love it when their grandmother takes them to the park after school. On good days they'll get ice-creams.

Now that she's 11 and has started secondary school, Rose likes to go shopping with her granny. "We have completely different tastes," she said, "but that just makes us both laugh. We love doing it together. One time she picked the frumpiest dress and the most stupid blouse with frills and bows and gushed that they'd look so pretty on me. Then, when she saw the look on my face, she just burst into giggles and said that was just the kind of outfit her mother used to make her wear!"

"Being a playmate seemed to be the role where grandmothers had most agency," said Cappellini. "They decided what activities to select and were creative in transforming some of the more ordinary aspects of the day into extraordinary occasions. This is because parental control over such activities seemed to be more relaxed, and were enjoyed simply as a way of 'having fun' together."

Most of her respondents would rather be able to be more spontaneous – to trust their own instincts rather than following a set schedule. But they were also aware that the idea of what makes a good childhood has changed so much from when they were bringing up their own children.

"So what we found was that participants were mostly aware of a shift in parenting culture: the growing pressure on children that have to learn new skills at a very young age. They compared this with their time as parents and could see the difference. They were more relaxed regarding the academic outcomes of the children as they saw this as a new trend in parenting."

The grandmothers I've interviewed agreed that they had allowed their own children far more freedom. Even primary-school kids would walk to school themselves; they'd be able to go to the shops, spend their own pocket money, play in the park without being supervised. Some worried that children who were constantly being watched and protected, having so many activities arranged for them, wouldn't learn to be independent and self-reliant. "Some have spoken about paranoid parenting," said Cappellini, "and the consequences of overprotecting children making them less confident and independent."

That is very much the view of psychologist Emily Edlynn, the author of the essential new parenting book *Autonomy-Supportive Parenting*. "Our children need to be more independent in childhood to grow into successful adults," she told *Good Housekeeping*. Autonomous children, she claims, do better in school, have better relationships and tend to be happier. So if parents are overprotective they could well be harming the development of their children, and their future. The practice of what she calls hypermonitoring became more pernicious during the pandemic. Intensive parenting is often driven by fear and anxiety, which the pandemic provided in abundance.

"Even as we move further away from the height of the pandemic," she said, "its effects on children continue to reveal themselves, including what appears to be kids' lagging independence. One New York mother told me her 7-year-old had no idea how to use a key to unlock a door – an adult was just always home to let them in. Another parent in Chicago shared that her 8-year-old son insists he's unable to spread peanut butter and jelly on bread by himself."

But even before the pandemic, parental hypermonitoring and supervision became the norm in the 2000s, and the evidence – in America at least – is now beginning to show. Edlynn reports that high school graduates are arriving at college unprepared for independent life. In a national poll conducted by the University of Michigan in 2019, parents acknowledged that their teenagers weren't ready for adulthood. A quarter of these parents blamed themselves, saying it was just faster or easier if they took on those responsibilities.

So maybe grandmothers should seize the initiative and instil that autonomy themselves? Why not break some of the rules in order to encourage children to think and act for themselves? I'd be all in favour of a more casual, loving regime. As long as you don't jeopardise safety – which, it seems, is all too easy, according to the complaints that crowd the advice columns.

"Today I was in the bathroom while she was getting them ready and I came out to find my one-year-old unsupervised in the living room," one anxious mother told Gransnet. "The door to the front hall was open and the baby gate on the stairs was open. So he had access to two flights of stairs. He's only just started climbing onto the couch etc. and loves it! So I obviously think leaving him unsupervised for several minutes with access to two flights of stairs is dangerous. That's why the baby gate is there. I tried to be calm and explain how fast he is and that he is not safe to go up or down steps yet, especially unsupervised. My mum didn't seem bothered. She said sorry but in a blasé kind of way."

"My mother is the typical grandma in that she lets our daughter do nearly anything she wants, won't tell her no, and hates to see her upset at all," another fretting mother told the advice website Slate. "She just watched both kids for the first time last week and we came home to huge bruises on the toddler's forehead and arm. My mother had put her on the couch, she had started running around, and my mother stepped away for a minute to pick up the baby, who had started crying. In that time, she fell off the side of the couch, and landed on her arm, also hitting her head."

Even the most assiduous granny will have pangs about the occasional careless moment: the day you boiled the kettle too close to the carrycot, or when you forgot the suncream, or when you let them on their scooters without helmets. I'd still recommend that we all relax a little. Watch the kids, of course, but most of all enjoy them – and love them.

After all, few of us could be quite as cavalier as the apocryphal Liverpool granny who happily fed neat Guinness to the new baby. When an appalled health visitor suggested that she should give him milk instead, she pointed defiantly at the baby's huge, strapping father. "He's done all right," she said, "and never had a tit in his mouth until he was courting."

Seven

Long-Distance Grannies

"It's the cuddles I miss the most," Linda told me. She lives in Hull but her granddaughter, who is also my granddaughter, is near London. Now there's a new baby, also near London. Linda sees them as often as she can, but that's never enough.

"We rely so much on Zoom," says Jill. She lives in London, while her two grandchildren live in Dublin. "It's a life-saver, but really it's a poor substitute for being there physically."

It's even more difficult for Jane. She's in Surrey, while her little granddaughter lives in New Zealand. "I visit when I can, but best of all was the time last year when my daughter brought her to stay with me for a couple of months," she said. "I really get to know the baby, to see her developing, to share all the feeding and, especially, the cuddles. But oh – it's so painful when they leave."

There are so many other bereft grandmothers like these all across the world, according to Selma Wasserman, author of *The Long Distance Grandmother*. She was inspired to write her book of advice by her own experience – her two grandsons live 400 miles away. She found that among her own close circle of friends, most also lived far from their grandchildren.

More than half of grandparents in the US have at least one grandchild who lives more than 200 miles away, according to a survey by AARP, formerly known as the American Association of Retired Persons. They reported that in 1999 just 26 per cent of grandparents only had grandkids who lived more than an hour away, while 34 per cent only had grandkids within an hour's drive and 39 per cent had a mix of grandkids near and far.

"There are no statistics on how many pining grannies there are out there, " wrote Sarah Iven in the *Daily Mail*, "but as the latest UN figures show, five million Brits now live abroad, and many more families within Britain live hundreds of miles apart, it's little surprise this is one of the most popular topics on Gransnet's advice forums."

Even a generation ago, far more families would have lived close to each other. "In the years when I was growing up," wrote Wasserman, "the extended family of three generations commonly lived quite close together. When I was very young my grandparents lived on the street floor of our rented two-family house and there was no differentiation between 'our' place and 'theirs'. I was as much with them as I was upstairs; perhaps even more."

Linda remembered how much she valued having her own parents living nearby when she was bringing up her own three sons. They would always drop in to see the grandparents, who were more than happy to babysit, or to take the children on outings. She's wistful about how much she feels she's missing that closeness. "Of course I love to visit," she said, "but I'm really looking forward to when they're older and can come and stay. I'd like to do normal things with them. I can't wait for Mila to be old enough to stay with me, for us to be at the kitchen table baking together. And I really look forward to gardening with her and showing her how to grow vegetables."

So many grandparents feel a real sense of loss, worrying, like Linda, that they will miss out on so many stages of development and won't be present for their milestones.

"I call it grandparent grief," Kerry Byrne told *Good Housekeeping*. She's a research scientist and founder of the organisation The Long-Distance Grandparent. "I hear from grandparents all the time who are struggling with this idea of knowing they want to support their adult children but feeling robbed of the relationship they looked forward to."

When Jane accepted that she wouldn't be able to do the usual things you associate with grandparents, she and her husband began to wonder what it means to be a grandparent. "We don't do any grandparenting things," he'd pointed out. They'll never have a chance to pop in, to babysit, to take grandchild on outings. "That really made me think about what grandparenting really is," Jane said. "I decided that it's not the day-to-day that matters. Far more important is the love and support, the memories, the special times you share. That's what I mean by grandparenting."

So how do women like Linda, and so many other long-distance grandmothers I've spoken to, maintain contact with the children and make sure they develop close relationships with them?

When my daughter became pregnant she set up a WhatsApp group just for the two grannies. "I valued that so much," Linda told me. "It was wonderful to feel involved at every stage, and since then we've continued to share so many messages and photos. And it's also brought our two families together, which is another huge bonus."

Jane also benefits from knowing and liking her daughter's in-laws in New Zealand. "It's a real comfort – they do all they can to make me feel welcome and involved when I go over there – although of course we can't manage that very often."

Visits are important, of course, although it can be upsetting if the baby doesn't recognise you at first. "Each time we'd have to start again and it would take a whole day for her to get used to us," said Linda. "Now that she's a bit older she adjusts much more quickly. I get lots of hugs, she'll hold my hand when we go for walks."

But her granddaughter was born during the first year of Covid-19, which made visits much more difficult. Who could forget those heartbreaking images of children waving through the windows at grandparents in care homes? In families that were separated by long distances, many grandmothers were terrified of losing touch.

Jill found there were some advantages, though. With all the spare time imposed by lockdown she would have long Zoom conversations with the grandchildren. She was able to read whole books to the older one, which made their bond much closer. As well as the regular calls and Zoom meetings, Jill makes a point of writing to each child. "It's so much more special to receive a card through the post. They both enjoy hearing about our life in London, and I like to cover lots of their interests."

I remember walking with Jill through the sculpture exhibition in Regent's Park in 2023. She would stop and snap any she thought her granddaughter would like, and send the photos in her next letter.

"I do make a point of finding things that might intrigue them. And you have to keep up with the changes. At the moment my grandson is into dinosaurs and the girls love dancing and mermaids. Who know what it'll be next? But I think it's important to introduce them to new ideas and new ways of thinking. I'm originally from America, they're Irish, and it's good for them to discover diversity, to be aware of different cultures."

She was also a long-distance granddaughter. Her parents moved round the world when she and her sisters were growing up, so she valued the letters from her grandparents. She has kept them all.

"The postal connection still endures as an important means of reaching out and making contact," agrees Selma Wasserman. "In an era when the art of letter writing is losing ground, it may be considered archaic to write; but, in fact, there is nothing quite like getting a real letter from someone you love."

For Betsy, writing to her grandchildren is especially important as she gets to see them so rarely. She lives in London, but has been separated from her grandchildren in America since their parents split up. For a while she was able to visit but it's becoming increasingly difficult, now that her son is back in the UK and her daughter-in-law won't let the children come to her. They're now teenagers, so she's hoping contact will be smoother as they become adults.

She does all she can to keep that close bond – by post. Ever since they were born she and her husband Martin have sent each child a postcard every week – and she maintains the habit even now. From very early on, when the younger child, Sophia, was born, she and Martin devised a very personal project for her. Martin loved limericks and enjoyed drawing, so each postcard would take the form of one letter, connected to a rhyme by Edward Lear and illustrated by Martin. When he became very ill Betsy encouraged him to continue with the drawings so that they could complete the alphabet before he died. So that's what they did. Although she can speak to the grandchildren only occasionally, she knows they value those weekly messages.

Nothing, though, can compare with seeing them in person. So the highlight of her year is the annual family get-together in Virginia, where she was brought up and where the extended family still lives. Except for the Covid-19 years she'd join everyone there, with her daughter and her grandchildren. This is always a special time for them all. The younger children love to see their big American cousins, and to play with them on the beach when everyone, for a brief time, could be carefree.

"It's so important for them to realise they're part of a big family," Betsy said. Like Linda, she also treasures her relationship with the other (American) grandma. "Their family may be fragmented, but they do have us both, as well as all their other relatives."

Betsy's plight is not unusual. According to the charity The Grandparents' Association, 42 per cent of British grandparents lose contact with their grandchildren after a son or daughter's relationship breaks down and, of these, one million are denied contact by one parent. Sarah Rainey wrote in the *Daily Mail* in 2015 that the mother will usually get custody, and would be legally entitled to move abroad, taking the children with her. In these cases the father and the grandparents will have no right to stop her, or to see the children. Rainey added that "since a 2001 ruling, when a judge allowed a divorced mother to move from England to New Zealand with her child, the tide of so-called 'virtual grandparents' has swelled. Their only contact with their grandchildren is online via email, Facebook or video calls on Skype." One couple resorted to the law to try to stop their daughter-in-law from leaving the country with the children after she and their son had divorced. They staked their life savings, £30,000, on the battle, but they lost, and now have to rely for contact on occasional video links.

In 2011, a government report recommended enshrining contact rights in law, though this has never been enacted. The 2014 *Children and Families Act simply states that* access for grandparents to their grandchildren should initially be sought through agreement with the parents or carers of the child. If this fails, the grandparent can seek the leave of the court, and, if successful, apply for a child arrangements order to agree access. This additional step is in place "to act as a filter to sift out those applications that are clearly not in the child's best interests", but in practice seems to be just one more cumbersome requirement for desperate, anguished grandparents.

In general there seems to be little appetite for considering the needs of grandparents. In 2023 the Italian Supreme Court decreed that children shouldn't be forced to see their grandparents. After a protracted battle in Milan, when grandparents were pitted against parents, the court finally ruled that visits should be up to the children themselves. That, in the land of powerful matriarchs and massively indulged children!

Too many grandparents have to endure this kind of separation, and the frustration of having so few rights. But there are so many other anxieties faced by long-distance grandmothers. Lucy has two grandchildren the UK, but her other two live on a kibbutz in Israel where she and her then husband brought up their own children. She frequently visits, but at times she worries about them. Her fears have increased since the Hamas atrocities of October 2023, followed by the war in Gaza. "I'm not so concerned about their physical safety," she said. "Their kibbutz is not near the conflict. But I do worry about their mental health, and I always have. It's never easy to know that just a few miles away are people who want to slit your throat. All I can think about is the terrible toll on human life on both sides – and of course the endless danger that my family and so many others are facing every day."

Like so many grandmothers and mothers she's well aware of that anguish and terror felt by families across the border in Gaza. Women's organisations like Israeli-based Women Wage Peace and Palestinian-based Women of the Sun and the long-established Women in Black all work together to campaign for peace. After the Hamas attack, Women Wage Peace posted an image of a bloodied dove on their social media feed and issued a statement calling for unity: "Every mother, Jewish and Arab, gives birth to her children to see them grow and flourish and not to bury them. That's why, even today, amid the pain and the feeling that the belief in peace has collapsed, we extend a hand in peace to the mothers of Gaza and the West Bank."

Amid the devastation of the war, a different kind of long-distance granny is making her own peace gesture. Shehnaz

Bakr, a 64-year-old grandma, was displaced from Gaza to Rafah during the war and now reaches out not to her own grandchildren but to those stranded across the border. She turns old products made out of wool into winter caps and dresses for Gazan children, knitting joy and warmth amidst the sounds of bombardment. Her granddaughter helps her, while children surround her waiting for their turn to get some warmth. Shehnaz's hope is for Palestine to be free.

Valya is another grandmother whose life has been upended by war. She has been living in London since the invasion of Ukraine in 2022. At first, she stayed with her two children as guests of a UK family. She felt very lucky that the couple who had opened their home to her were kind, friendly and incredibly thoughtful. They'd even secured school places for the children before they arrived and did all they could to make them feel at home. But the transition wasn't easy. Nikita, who is now 11, would cry himself to sleep every night, missing his friends, his happier life and, most of all, his grandmother Nadiya. She had chosen to stay in Ukraine with her son Viktor and his family. Like all men over 17, he has to remain, and she didn't want to leave the country they loved.

Valya worries constantly about her own mother, still in Ukraine. "She's moved from Kyiv, where we all lived, and is now in her country house in Chernihav where she's safer," said Valya. "Although nowhere is really safe. Although she's 200 kilometres from Kyiv there's still danger, not just from nearby bombing but from the pieces that fall over quite large areas." So many others she knows in this country are fretting about the precarious situation of their families caught up in the conflict.

Valya remembers how much the children used to love being with their grandmother. They spent a lot of time with her, and especially enjoyed staying in the country house during school holidays, where they could enjoy the fresh air and the freedom. Now they stay in touch with phone and video calls, at least once a day. But that's no substitute for the easy closeness they used to have. "My mother misses doing normal things with the children, having fun, seeing them developing. She would so love to hug them."

Valya is clearly a strong and resourceful woman. She's found somewhere to live and has a good job. "It's no good wishing things were different. You just have to adapt. And for me the most important thing is to take care of the children and to make a new life for them for as long as we're here." As for her mother? "Every time we speak she says how much she wants the war to be over, for everything to go back to what it was. And to have us home again."

Juliet has a rather different concern: she fears losing emotional connection with her grandchild. They were very close for the first few years, until her daughter's family moved to the United States. Juliet still visited as often as she could. But when Tracy was 11 she started to feel uncomfortable with her growing adolescent body, and around that time announced that she was "non-binary". Juliet was baffled by her choice but was determined not to let that weaken what had always been a strong bond. "It just felt rather alien to me," she said. "Her parents were very supportive, which was quite comforting. But it took me a long time to get used to referring to Tracy as 'they', and to call her by her (fortunately) neutral middle name, Robin." Eventually Robin made the decision to transition completely, and yet again Juliet had to adjust to this new yet very familiar young person. "Now my grandchild is a rather beautiful 16-year-old, but with a deep, gravelly voice and the beginnings of facial hair. It's been quite an adjustment but I'm so happy that we've managed to stay close. I still love Robin as much as ever, and always will."

Jane was just as adamant. "I will love her no matter what," she said. "People often tell me how hard it must be to live so far from Eve, but I try not to think of it that way. It may be hard, I suppose, but it's also a joy, glorious, and I'm conscious that I must make the most of it all." She offered an unexpected piece of advice for other long-distance grandmothers. "Communication. I'm always looking for opportunities and possibilities, while my husband sees reality and challenges. So it's really important that we've been able to discuss how to handle this new relationship in our lives. I realise I can't just fly off to New Zealand whenever I want to, and he's better at planning what would work for us."

Lucy values her frequent visits because although she is in constant touch with her children and grandchildren, online communication can never replace being with them. Like Jane, she tries to organise long visits. "Short stays are not good," she said. "It takes time for the children to get to know you again, especially the younger ones, who will always be shy at first. You need to create opportunities to get to know them again, to communicate, break the ice and spend time doing normal things like going for walks together or sharing meals."

Lucy found that as the children grew older communication became trickier. The eldest, a boy of 14, is going through that universal teenage boy phase of saying very little. But even though he's often unresponsive she thinks it's important to keep the door open – sending him pictures that she thinks might interest him, making sure he knows she's there for him.

"Be patient," agreed Linda. "Always be available if you're needed, and stay in contact no matter what."

Jill learned from her own parents and grandparents how patient you need to be in your dealings with the new generation. "I'm aware that I'm not going to be the most important person in their lives. But I do want them to know I'm always there for them. Love and happiness are what really matters."

That, of course, is the uniting factor for all the women I've spoken to. No matter how far away they are, how difficult it can be to meet or to talk, how painful the separations can be, it's love that keeps them going, fuels the difficult times and still fills them with joy.

The Last Words of My English Grandmother
by William Carlos Williams

There were some dirty plates
and a glass of milk
beside her on a small table
near the rank, disheveled bed—

Wrinkled and nearly blind
she lay and snored
rousing with anger in her tones
to cry for food,

Gimme something to eat—
They're starving me—
I'm all right I won't go
to the hospital. No, no, no

Give me something to eat
Let me take you
to the hospital, I said
and after you are well

you can do as you please.
She smiled, Yes
you do what you please first
then I can do what I please—

Oh, oh, oh! she cried
as the ambulance men lifted
her to the stretcher—
Is this what you call

making me comfortable?
By now her mind was clear—
Oh you think you're smart
you young people,

she said, but I'll tell you
you don't know anything.
Then we started.
On the way

we passed a long row
of elms. She looked at them
awhile out of
the ambulance window and said,

What are all those
fuzzy-looking things out there?
Trees? Well, I'm tired
of them and rolled her head away.

Eight

Her Upstairs: Live-in Grannies

When Maggie's son, wife and two children returned to the UK after a couple of years abroad they had nowhere to live, so she had no hesitation in inviting them to move in with her. She and her husband had always run an open house, welcoming friends from all over the world. After he died she continued the tradition. Sam and family were offered two rooms in her North London house, alongside Sophie, daughter of an old friend who was studying in London. There was still room for occasional visitors from abroad, too.

"It can be chaotic," Maggie admitted. "At least it was a bit easier once I'd had a second bathroom put in, and a dishwasher." But although it was quite a crowded household, she wouldn't have wanted it any other way. One big advantage is that they usually eat together, all squashed round the huge kitchen table, and everyone shares the cooking. Sophie likes to prepare incredibly healthy vegan suppers, while Maggie's daughter-in-law Tatiana creates wonderful Brazilian stews.

The house is close to the children's school, and Maggie is often on hand to pick them up, and to be around if anyone is ill. She's happy to help out and loves having such a close relationship with the children, although she does admit she has little time to herself. But while she rarely complains, her son worries that they may be exploiting her, and feels ashamed sometimes that they rely on her so much. At least they're able to talk about any conflicts – and that, says Maggie, is crucial.

The family's living arrangements are becoming increasingly common. There was a time, not long ago, when newly married couples would move in with his or her parents. Those arrangements often caused friction. But over the past century family dynamics have changed considerably, most dramatically with the radical housing reforms after the Second World War. Slum clearance meant tight-knit family networks were broken up as young couples moved out into the new estates.

Lately, however, families are beginning to share homes once again. With the rocketing price of housing, young couples are increasingly having to depend on their parents' hospitality. The number of households with three generations living together has risen from 325,000 in 2001 to 1.8 million in 2023.

Dr Gemma Burgess, acting director of the Cambridge Centre for Housing and Planning Research, has interviewed dozens of multigenerational families. "What struck us the most was the high level of trust and the absolute lack of any financial or inheritance planning, or any legal structure for their living arrangements," Burgess says. "People had invested their life savings in a house with their grown-up children and not had their names put on the deeds: 'Oh, we trust them – it will be all right, they'll look after us.'"

Some ministers have recognised the value of this way of living. In a speech in 2004, when he was the Liberal Democrat justice minister, Simon Hughes suggested that Britain should follow the example set by Asian and African immigrants of caring for their elder relations instead of "forcing" them into care homes. He said that too many elderly people were being "neglected" by their families and endured a "much less happy ending" to their lives than they should. He suggested that "immigrant cultures" understand the importance of "sacrifices" and a responsibility to "look after your family to the end".

Jeremy Hunt, whose wife is Chinese, suggested in 2013, when he was the health secretary, that the British should follow the example of the Chinese and look after their elderly relatives in their homes. After a BBC survey found that many elderly people in Britain felt lonely, Hunt branded the findings a source of "national shame" and said we should learn from Asian cultures where there was "reverence and respect for older people" and "residential care is a last rather than a first option".

More than 6 per cent of British households – a total of around 1.8 million people – are multi-generational. In the UK, people from Black, Asian and Minority Ethnic (BAME) communities are more likely than their White peers to be living in such groups.

Rabnawaz Akbar lives in Manchester, with his wife, his 85-year-old mother and three of his daughters – Salma, 30, Asma, 28, and Farah 17. The local politician has two other adult children: a son living in London and another daughter in Newcastle. According to a CNN report by Zamira Rahim, families like his faced real dilemmas when Covid-19 arrived – especially when government advice was to isolate vulnerable elderly relatives.

"Certainly those from the Muslim faith and in South Asian [groups], there is this belief that you've got a duty to look after your older parents," Rabnawaz Akbar said. "Most of the taking care of older relatives is done by family – it's beneficial to society – but sadly during the Covid-19 crisis, that has become a negative, because of how the virus spreads among people living in multi-generational households."

Akbar told Rahim that his own family has been forced to implement stringent routines to cope with the pandemic. His daughter Salma is an optometrist. "She sees patients all day long. She comes home and has to be careful around my mum," Akbar said, explaining that Salma tries to minimise the risk of contamination by changing her clothes immediately on returning home.

The fear of transmitting the virus to their loved ones has driven some younger people to leave their family homes. Saima Afzal, a 49-year-old British Asian woman living in Blackburn, said her son and granddaughter lived away from the family home for three weeks because of concerns about her health. Now that her son has moved back in, she is partly responsible for the childcare of her four-year-old granddaughter Elia Rose.

"It works out – between the two of us we maintain the household income," she said, adding that being around her granddaughter had kept her cheerful, even while coping with illness and the pandemic. "We're so, so careful. I feel that I'm so lucky that I live in this household. Yes, there are risks, of course. But if I didn't have my son and my family support network I don't know what I'd have done."

Multigenerational families are more ingrained in different parts of the world. Canada has seen a 40 per cent rise in multigenerational households, and about 64 million Americans – about 20 per cent of the population – have multiple generations under one roof, according to the Pew Research Center.

In India, particularly outside cities, young women are expected to live with their husband's family when they get married. The journalist Perminder Khatkar spent 15 years living with her husband's parents. In a BBC Radio 4 piece in 2009, she investigated the benefits – and the difficulties. "For many Asian women in the UK, living with their husband's family leads to arguments, from petty squabbles over not washing the dishes, to more serious disagreements which can turn nasty," she explained to *BBC News* magazine. She cited the example of Sandeep, 27, from Birmingham, who moved in with the in-laws as soon as she got married and found it very stressful. "It was constant nerves, 'shall I do this, shall I do that?' You don't know how to behave."

Thirty-nine-year-old Humera, a teacher from Walsall, empathised strongly with that sense of bewilderment when she moved in with her husband's parents. "I remember standing in the bathroom and thinking, 'What have I done?'" Humera rebelled against the traditional view that the daughter-in-law is expected to cook, clean, do all the washing and ironing, and hold down a full-time job.

Similar frustrations were described by this Bengali contributor to Mumsnet, who lives with her husband's mother. "My husband and I are very happy together and have a beautiful little boy. My mother-in-law is also a lovely person, well-educated and working as a professional. But even so, I really don't like living like this, I feel like I have had my choices in life taken from me, from where to live to how I live. I have to think twice before I invite anyone to stay or visit (even my family), as she feels like she has to do the whole Asian cooking thing and it's too much work for her as she's not in the best health. I also find it stressful that she always seems to observe my parenting. I feel like I'm constantly under supervision or something!"

Another Mumsnet contributor shared her experience of living with the in-laws. "The whole environment and people became toxic very quick. I was treated and spoken to really badly whilst I lived with them. They expected me to do all the housework and disagreed with me having a career. My husband and I decided not to give up on each other and moved out."

According to Burgess, young married women in these joint families are more vulnerable to abuse and suffer higher rates of depression and even suicide. She identified a pattern of families who had settled in Britain reverting to gender stereotypes. "What was obvious," she says, "was if you are the middle-aged woman living in one of those households then the burden of all the domestic work falls to you."

Even so, Khatkar does recognise the advantages of the arrangement. "Going to live in a ready-made home, having free childcare and sharing the mortgage and household bills does make financial sense for those trying to get on the property ladder."

Women like these may have difficulty dealing with a dominant, highly possessive mother-in-law. But experiences can be quite different when a couple moves in with *her* parents.

Anita discovered that she was going to have a baby just when her husband Tariq had been accepted onto an MBA programme in Spain. So she moved into her parents' house when her daughter was just two weeks old. During the months that Tariq was studying, Anita said, it was really helpful to have a base and reliable support from her parents, Mary and Gordon. When she returned to work part-time while Tariq was still in Spain, her mother provided childcare for one day a week, which was invaluable. Anita is also grateful that living at home has also meant she and Tariq can occasionally go out for dinner or have a "date night".

After Tariq completed his course he came back to join her in her parents' house. "Our set-up is quite flexible and we don't have set schedules," Anita said. "We probably eat together around 50 per cent of the time, but trying to plan timings and meals for a two-year-old while making sure everyone in the house is catered for is sometimes difficult. Even so, my mum cooks for us all a lot of the time, and will readily do dinner for my daughter if I and my husband have to work late.

"My mum and dad both say regularly that they love having us living with them, and especially love the time they have with our daughter and the relationships that have grown out of spending so much time together," Anita said. "They are very present in her life – she runs into their room in the morning full of excitement and shares lots of little games and jokes with each of them, which is magical. I feel very fortunate for this and know I will look back on it with huge gratitude.

"Nevertheless, my mum will also admit that she finds it hard at times and I think not having clear boundaries can be especially difficult (such as me suddenly asking if she's free for half an hour rather than having to request her time in advance). I know she wants to help and struggles to say no, and when the request is coming from inside the house, it's a lot more difficult to just say, 'I can't' unless it's demonstrable that she can't.

"I'm aware that my parents were used to having a quiet house after all their children left, and now in their seventies and eighties, it is a lot to ask of them. There is of course lots more 'stuff' in the house with the three of us being there, and containing the mess of a toddler (and parents who could be tidier) is not always easy."

How does Tariq feel about living with his parents-in-law?

"Actually, I would say that he has dealt with it far better than I have. While there will of course be odd moments of disagreement, he is very good at taking feedback without it becoming personal and will remove himself from situations if he feels space is needed. It has also been interesting – and quite useful at times – to have Tariq's insight into my relationship with my parents and the dynamics between us. He has joked that everyone should have to live with their in-laws for a bit as it provides such insight into who their spouse is and where their behaviours/habits/idiosyncrasies etc come from."

But living in such a crowded house, with so little privacy, is especially hard for Tariq. He is sometimes frustrated at his lack of autonomy. "For example," Anita said, "if he wanted to make changes to the space, or 'replace the crappy iron', he feels like he'd have to get 'permission' from my parents first, and then potentially me as the person who's taken more charge of how we live in the space and whose childhood home it is. Whereas if we were in our own home, he'd be able to respond to his own sense of need more immediately and just buy a new iron (or whatever). I think the sense for him of having these restrictions and needing to get approval, even if in reality it doesn't limit much, can be difficult. I'm trying to consider more, as I often take his easy nature as a sign that he doesn't need anything and perhaps underestimate the importance of these seemingly little elements of autonomy in a space that isn't his."

On the whole, though, everyone agrees that living together has had fantastic advantages. One of the reasons, Anita suggested, is that Tariq gets on so well with Mary and Gordon. But not all husbands have had such positive experiences. Writing for the magazine *Asian Living*, Umbreen Ali said his self-esteem suffered as a result of living with his wife's family. "As if my wife's constant fights with her mum weren't bad enough, the atmosphere was always tense," he wrote. "I was constantly reminded how lucky I am that I am not paying the bills or the mortgage because when I moved over from Pakistan, I couldn't get a job. The constant taunts and jibes made me feel inept, like I had failed in life. I don't feel like a man. In our culture, men who live with their in-laws are seen as failures."

Such tensions are certainly not confined to these communities. Living with the bride's parents used to be very common in Britain, and probably gave rise to that gold standard of English humour: the mother-in-law joke.

The archetypal mother-in-law – bossy, interfering, disapproving, nosy and curmudgeonly – is immortalised by the matchless Les Dawson and features as the butt in his most famous routines. She is the woman so formidable she cancels her own funeral. She's Mussolini with knickers: the constant tormentor of long-suffering husbands everywhere. No wonder that when she tells Les she's going to dance on his grave, he's delighted: "Good, I'm being buried at sea." No wonder that when he took her to Madame Tussaud's Chamber of Horrors one of the attendants said, "Keep her moving, sir, we're stock-taking." "You always know when the mother-in-law is coming to stay," Les would confide, "because the mice throw themselves on the traps."

To many young men, trapped and emasculated by the critical presence of an all-powerful dictator, the mother-in-law as ogre would be a recognisable type. The jokes spring from terror rather than hatred, just as they did in the mediaeval bacchanalia. Following the same principle, in order to neutralise her power and authority Les actually becomes his own mother-in-law.

But what happens when it's the grandmother who moves in with one of her children?

Writing in *Verily* magazine, Monica Burke extolled the advantages of living with a beloved grandmother. "It's tempting to focus on the challenges of old age," she maintained, "but this new phase comes with unique joys as well." She had always adored her grandmother, and had loved visiting her. But as she grew older and more frail, her parents decided to invite her to live with them and their four daughters.

"When Grammy first came to live with us, she was a huge help to our family. She championed laundry duty, cooked whenever my parents went out of town, and drove us to and from school. She would take my sisters and me to the movies and out mini-golfing. If I ever had a bad dream, I would climb into bed with her and fall asleep instantly. She basically helped to raise me and my sisters.

"There are hard memories too. There were tough conversations, like when a close call with opposing traffic led us to decide that Gram should not drive at night anymore. There are now more limits on what she can do on her own. For example, she used to stay at home by herself when we left for long trips but now stays with our aunt and uncle in case of emergency.

"As the years have gone on, I've come to understand that living with us has been good for my grandmother's mental and physical health – she still comes up and down the stairs every day and keeps busy with chores, and she is always eager to talk and hear about what is new in our lives. She says that staying in the know about our love lives is what keeps her young!"

But that's not how it was for one contributor to Ageing Care. "My grandmother moved in with us almost a year ago," she wrote. "She did raise me, so it's like having my mother here. Since living with us she has been beyond anxious, rude, mean, intrusive and so much more. Our relationship is nonexistent and I don't know what to do. She parents my daughter and interjects when she shouldn't. When I confront her, she cries and puts it on me. I'm trying my best and she's really the only family I have. I don't know what to do. We emptied her house out because we planned on her staying with us but I feel trapped and like it's ruining my marriage and my life."

Conflicts like these were acutely dramatised in the BBC's 2013 documentary *Granny's Moving In*. Paddy Wivell's film featured Sue and Phil Carol, an East London couple, who were preparing for Sue's 83-year-old mother Peggy to live with them, just as their own daughters were beginning to move out. Peggy suffered from dementia and lived a determinedly independent lifestyle, going into town every day and coming home late. "She's got a mind of her own," said Sue. "You can tell a ten-year-old what to do, how can you do that with you own mother?"

But as Peggy's dementia progressed, Sue and Phil found it increasingly difficult to cope with her erratic behaviour. Occasional rows developed into endless screaming matches, while Peggy became more and more confused. "It's a nightmare," Sue confessed at one point. Eventually, she and Phil decided they couldn't manage any more. They sold their house and bought a new one, complete with its own granny annexe. The film ended with all three of them hoping that Peggy would be able to cope with her new freedom, and that family harmony would be restored.

This situation is becoming increasingly common. When Barbara was diagnosed with Alzheimer's her daughter Clare and husband Richard took it for granted that she must move in with the family. Although there were difficulties at times, said Clare, there were so many advantages. The two young boys had fun with their grandma at first. She'd tell them stories and play cards with them. As her condition worsened they learned to be patient with her. They loved the way she'd raucously cheer on her favourite Manchester City, even when she could no longer quite follow the rules. When Barbara did eventually move to a care home, the boys would regularly visit, and always valued their time with her.

A more intense bond between grandmother and grandchild is dramatised in Jenny Downham's novel *Unbecoming*, in which the Todd family is disrupted by the arrival of grandmother Mary. Although suffering from Alzheimer's, Mary remains the spirited, rebellious, irresponsible woman she has always been. Teenager Katie, ostracised by her friends and alienated from her strict mother as she struggles to come to terms with her sexuality, finds herself drawn to Mary. She loves hearing about her colourful life and increasingly cares for her as Mary's condition deteriorates. But looking after her isn't easy. Mary often runs away as her memory begins to fade, and sometimes she doesn't know where she is or how to manage the simplest tasks.

Downham explains that her own mother had Alzheimer's and became very unwell and died while she was writing *Unbecoming*. "I hope I was a better carer and daughter as a result of writing this book. Certainly, I found it very cathartic to try and imagine how my mum might have been feeling as she faced the erosion of her memories. There's a lot of my mum in Mary."

Whether it's grannies moving in with the family, or young couples coming home, there are bound to be problems. The solution, according to Manisha Patel, a senior partner with PRP Architects, is for housing to be designed for multigenerational families – like the project she has designed for a new neighbourhood in East London, with others in the pipeline. "Young people can't get on the housing ladder, so you get kids coming home, families growing who can't afford to move," she told *The Observer*. "You're getting loft conversions and extensions, and people are losing their independence. This is where the multigenerational house comes in."

Her design is for a three-storey townhouse with a separate two-storey annexe connected by a courtyard, each with its own front door – a typology, in architectural jargon. "By having these new typologies, they can encourage communities to stay together. You don't have to move away," says Patel.

Manisha Patel is determined to create more options for families. Her latest idea is connectable flats, linked through the kitchen area. "It almost becomes the heart of the place where you connect together. But you also have your own independence, you have your own access to your flat, and you could separate the flats if you want to move out."

For many families, this seems to be the answer. Lucy shares a house with her daughter Libby, Libby's partner Alison, and their two children. "When I first knew that Libby and Alison were together I was quite taken aback. I hadn't known any lesbians before and it took some getting used to. But they are so much in love, so very happy, that it all now seems quite normal."

Libby and Alison had been together for about 15 years before they decided to have children. And they were very lucky that they were able to use the same sperm donor, which means that Ella, now twelve, and Bertie, who is eight, are half-siblings.

Nine years ago, when Ella was three, they all decided to buy a house together. At first, while building work was going on, they really were all together all of the time. And that wasn't ideal. No one felt comfortable living so closely and with so little privacy. But there were advantages, too.

Lucy still misses those weeks when they used to eat together, taking it in turns to cook. Now they have two independent households, but share the garden and laundry room. What makes it work is their openness and willingness to talk about any conflicts or problems.

First of all, they agreed that they would need to discuss rules of behaviour and division of expenses. "We got through this period, and ever since, by discussing any problems or niggles as they arose and deciding how to act. We had a chat about the things that we found irritating or offensive, and realised that actively interfering in each other's lives and lifestyles had to be avoided, although I and they do bring up concerns and discuss them."

It's great for the family to have Lucy on hand – especially if one of the children is ill, or for babysitting and during the holidays. Ella is now at secondary school, but Lucy often picks Bertie up from school. What is even more important than the convenience of having a grandma on hand is that they all appreciate the close bond they have with Lucy. She regards both children as her grandchildren, and treats Alison as another daughter.

At the same time, though, Lucy really values her independence. "The children know that in my part of the house they must follow my rules. They are not allowed to enter my area without permission, even – or especially – if I am not at home. In their part of the house they must do as their parents expect, and I remind them of that if I am looking after them."

But she does value being with the children. "They do come in a lot, even though the mums do try to ration their times. Living with them keeps me young. I love showing them all the things I love to do, especially being in the outdoors, gardening, going for walks. I like to tell them stories about my own childhood, which they seem to enjoy. And I like to see what they find interesting."

There's another advantage for Lucy. "I'm not very sociable, and tend to find social interaction exhausting. So it's good to be surrounded by people I feel comfortable with. And there is no doubt that life together enriches all our lives.

When Tess's husband died a few years ago, she was left with a large house. So she converted the house so that her daughter Billie, partner Ben and three little boys could have their own flat upstairs while she lived downstairs with her beloved garden. "It's lovely having them so close," she said, "without ever feeling we're on top of each other."

Like Lucy, Tess makes it quite clear that she needs her privacy, and doesn't want the boys feeling they can crash into her place whenever they want. And their mum is even stricter than she is about respecting boundaries.

One difficulty, Tess said, is that the upstairs flat doesn't have a separate staircase to the garden. So the boys have to go through Tess's kitchen to go out. That can be frustrating for Billie, who would love them to be able to enjoy the garden without bothering Tess. But at least, Tess reflected, it means that she, rather than her daughter, has to put up with the results of muddy boots trailing through her house.

Of course the boys do visit quite a lot, and Tess spends a lot of time with them. She looks after the toddler once a week and often picks up the boys from school. "I just love being a grandma," she told me. "It's so much easier than being a mum. And it's great to be able to read with them, tell them stories, watch them develop. I enjoy taking them on outings – the zoo, galleries, or even just a ride on the bus." She's always finding new ways to amuse them.

There are relatively few conflict zones, although Tess and Billie don't always agree about treats. Tess disapproves of how Billie is happy to give her children chewy sweets – even though, as Tess admits, she herself has always loved them. I remember the time she told me that sour Skittles were too good for children. Now she's worried that too many sweets are bad for them. But Billie in turn is concerned at the amount of crisps and Wotsits that Tess will happily hand round. When she sees the boys she's always armed with crunchy snacks.

Tess and Billie find their disagreements quite funny, often joking about who's the real mother in this family. In fact, Tess said, she, Billie and Ben are all very open about any difficulties that arise. It's so important, she said, to talk about them. Lucy also emphasised how vital it is to discuss any problems and to find solutions together.

Anita agreed. "We have recently started having regular house meetings to discuss any issues and find more harmonious ways of living alongside one another. This is still in its infancy but I think is a really important space for us all to be able to voice how we feel and to better understand one another's needs."

Nine

Chicken Soup and Samosas

Bubbe's chicken soup. Family gatherings round the table for Sunday lunch at Nana's house. A Hindu granny presiding over a Diwali feast. All over the world, food is that most sacred grandmother ritual: the ultimate gift of love.

"My granny Goodson was touched with a kind of genius in the kitchen," the writer Rachel Cooke told *The Observer*. "She made her own flaky pastry – imagine it!" Her book *Cooking and Eating* is rich with her memories of the comfort and love she always associated with her grandmothers. She recalls the precious times she would visit her granny Goodson. As soon as she arrived, tea would be already on the table.

"This was a proper high tea and always the same. It began with cold ham with salad (butter lettuce and tomatoes only) and salad cream on the side, and was followed by as much cake, shortbread etc. as you could possibly eat (there were no limits)… Staying with my granny was like being at a spa, except every treatment comprised a meal or (if we were between meals) some other tempting foodstuff.

"She had a morbid fear that someone might be hungry and would do anything to assuage it, mostly by making sure it had no chance to get going in the first place. Her questions were delightfully wheedling. 'Would you just like a little biscuit?' 'Could you manage a sandwich?' 'Are you sure you've had enough?'"

Grandmothers all across the world are just as passionate about feeding the family and making sure they have enough. The reason, according to the writer Anindita Ghose, is that food is the simplest, most direct, most universal expression of love. "'Have you eaten?' Indian mothers ask their children and husbands when they return home," Ghose wrote in *The Guardian*. "The 19th-century Japanese writer Natsume Sōseki is said to have encouraged his students to translate 'I love you' to 'The moon is beautiful, isn't it?' Its literal phrasing was too direct for the Japanese. 'Have you eaten?' is Sōseki's wisdom for Indians."

Tea, Ghose explained, is more than a drink, more than a meal. It's a ritual of love.

"If we visited two homes the same evening, we had to eat twice, so as to not offend the host. If it was a planned visit, the accompaniments were usually prepared at home. My grandmother's tea-time specialities were the kucho gojas and koraishutir kochuri (fried bread stuffed with peas).

"My gran most definitely used food as a form of love," wrote Feliz Hall in the *Cincinnati Mom Collective*, a local newsletter. "Like many grandmas, when we walked through her door, she insisted something yummy was in our bellies before we walked back out. If she knew we were coming, she made dependable favorites for the person coming." At Thanksgiving, Feliz remembered, "she would prepare from early in the morning until it was time to eat. My grandfather loved Thanksgiving. We had long tables full of food, punch, and desserts ... all hand-made. My last memory of my grandfather was Thanksgiving, attempting to eat the food my grandma had prepared even though cancer had stolen his appetite: *his way of showing her love back.*"

Andrew Flouzi, in *MEL Magazine*, extolled not just the wonders of his Persian grandmother's cooking, but the world of senses and memories it evoked.

"There is no good English translation for the Persian term *dastpokht*. Literally, it translates to 'hand cooking,' but its meaning is more akin to 'style of cooking' or 'mastery of cooking.' The term is, by definition, person specific, and it intends that the food created by the individual's hands is, by extension of their being, unique. It's also the only possible way to explain why my Persian grandmother's cooking— her *dastpokht*—is, for me, singular, because describing it to you is like trying to describe a ghost with any level of certainty. Sure, I could start by referencing some of the rich, uniquely Persian flavors and ingredients, like crushed, roasted walnuts simmering in turmeric-coated chopped onions and reduced in pomegranate molasses. I could also attempt to describe some of the scents, like that of her jeweled rice, which tantalizes once the butter and the cloves have reached critical mass. But none of it would really matter, because scientifically speaking, the greatness of her cooking goes so far beyond the simple spectrum of palatability."

Most of us, like Flouzi, have a memory of a food that takes us back to childhood. One reason that these memories are so vivid, according to Susan Whitbourne, professor of psychological and brain sciences at the University of

Massachusetts, is that they involve all five senses. "So when you're that thoroughly engaged with the stimulus it has a more powerful effect," she explains. "You're not just using your sight, or just your taste, but all the senses and that offers the potential to layer the richness of a food memory."

Our senses and survival tactics aren't the only elements at play when it comes to food memories. The situation – where you were, who you were with, what the occasion was – adds power to our nostalgic taste memories. "Food memories feel so nostalgic because there's all this context of when you were preparing or eating this food, so the food becomes almost symbolic of other meaning," Whitbourne says. "A lot of our memories as children, it's not so much the apple pie, for example, but the whole experience of being a family, being nourished, and that acquires a lot of symbolism apart from the sensory quality."

In *Gran Dishes: Recipes and Stories from Grandmothers of the World*, Mina Holland, one of the authors, remembers that whenever she visited her granny, "I always asked for kedgeree: all buttery onions and milky rice and smoky haddock and plenty of hard boiled eggs from toothless-Fred-down-the-road's hens. In that oft-cited Proustian way, each time I had it, I'd not only appreciate that portion, but reappreciate portions past.... . Her kedgeree, and many other things she cooked, seasoned my childhood with salt, fat and love, and made food into so much more than fuel – it took on an imaginative quality. Dishes and tastes and the smell of things cooking became associated with people and stories, places and moments."

Anastasia Miari, another of the book's authors, agreed that for her Yiayia, food is, quite simply, love. "Feeding our family is how she shows she loves us. Our meals together as a family are characterised with shouty disputes and wild cackles of laughter (often from her). The food is simple, made up of Yiayia's own produce, and never anything less than delicious. From Yiayia I have inherited this need to feed, to make mealtimes a social occasion for mutual connection. This project started with my wanting to share the special recipes that take me back to a place where I have felt most loved, at my grandmother's dining table."

"Food is more than nutrition," writes Katherine Moss, of the charity Migrateful. "When we cook we create, learn about our history, customs and discover our identity. Sharing food is sharing our inheritance, it is a language we all speak and the best medium to bridge the gap between communities."

Migrateful, founded in 2017, seeks to use the power of food to integrate refugees and asylum seekers arriving in the UK into the community. The act of cooking and sitting down together to have a family-style dinner provides the comfort of traditional tastes and smells, and offers connections between different groups. Refugees are supported, encouraged and trained to lead cookery classes, share their traditional cuisine and heritage to make connections. They develop menus based on their personal family recipes, share the social status behind each recipe or the cultural importance of serving a dish in certain circumstances.

Food provides a powerful connection with your own roots. The novelist Margaret Wilkerson Sexton credited her grandmother with introducing her to her own Creole heritage. Especially the food. "She was known for her cooking, her fried catfish, potato salad and jelly cakes. Her specialities were shrimp etouffee, red beans and rice, gumbo, stuffed mirlitons, jambalaya and pralines," she recalled in *The Observer*. Now that she has a daughter of her own it's the food they share that brings back her beloved grandmother. ""She helps me chop the yellow and green onions, roots through the pantry for bay leaves. When we're done, I watch her eat before I taste the food myself. It feels like there's something I'm fishing for that I can't name."

The novelist Howard Jacobson told me that his grandmother connected him to his Lithuanian heritage and to a past way of living. "She was a peasant," he said. "She looked like a peasant, she thought like a peasant, she had the superstitions of a peasant. She was from somewhere else." In his memoir *Mother's Boy*, he describes his adored grandmother taking him to the kosher butcher, "where impossibly complex negotiations about the age and cuts of meat invariably ended in her buying just a chicken. Or, rather, a hen, for a hen made the best of all chicken soups… . After the butcher's the shops we spent most time in were those that sold that soft, seemingly pre-digested baby bread we call challah, bagels, chopped and fried fish balls, herring, liver and tasteless cheese."

Musician David Gordon-Shute also associates his grandmother's food with her own past. "Both my grandparents were German/Jewish refugees who emigrated to the UK in 1936. My grandmother found herself one day at breakfast in a hotel on holiday with her sister and her sister's husband in Germany and were the only people present not wearing Nazi uniform. They made the decision to leave the country. The story goes that they arrived in the UK on 5th November and, because of all the fireworks, thought that the war had already started.

"My grandmother then met and married a fellow Jewish/German emigré in the UK and they managed a pretty good life here. She was not a very good cook but her one contribution to Christmas lunch every year was an amazing red cabbage which she cooked in the classic Jewish way. She died a number of years ago but I still try and recreate it when we host Xmas at home.

"The other thing that she did for my two sisters and me when we were growing up was arrive on Christmas day at 7.30am (or earlier if we were up and had already rung her to say, 'Where are you?') On arrival, she would place three decorative trays down and adorn them with Pfefferkuchen, satsumas, Lebkuchen, Bunter Teller and marzipan. All was bought at huge expense from the German Food Centre. My grandmother would complain about the hassle of having to make a special trip every year as well as the expense. Of course, shopping online makes these things easier and cheaper but I am sure that she would still find something to go on about. It was one of her endearing features."

Nostalgia for Granny's cooking brings a special comfort, representing the continuity of cultural traditions and identities.

"Taste memories tend to be the strongest of associative memories that you can make," psychologist Hadley Bergstrom told *HuffPost*. That is why food is such a powerful trigger of nostalgia, reinforcing associations with Grandma, with family, with childhood, and with home. "That's the nature of food memories," Bergstrom explains. "They aren't just based on the facts, or our need for survival, but are shaped by the context – the company, the situation and the emotions involved.

"My step-mom always recounts how great her grandmother's vanilla pudding was when she made it for her as a kid. She, at 57 years old, has been trying to recreate it since she was old enough to be cooking in a kitchen. It's a flavour she can practically taste through her memory of that dish, but one that she has not been able to reproduce successfully. And it's because she can't recreate the context. She can make great vanilla pudding, but she can't go back in time to the excitement she felt as a child for being given such a treat, by a person who was such a loving and nurturing force in her life."

Perhaps the most triumphant example of the power of Grandmother's cooking is the worldwide sensation Mastanamma. She rocketed to fame after, in 2016, her nephew filmed her cooking a mouth-watering aubergine curry, and posted the video on YouTube. At the time she was 105 years old. Over the next two years, she became the star of a YouTube channel with an audience of more than a million subscribers, and over 200 million views.

"Hordes of fans from around the world watched Mastanamma's pared-down cooking tips on making spicy shrimp powder and 'delicious cabbage'," reported Kai Schultz in the *New York Times*. "Mastanamma peeled ginger with her thumbs, stored bird eggs in her sari and posed for pictures with lamb heads. She made it all, barking out orders to subordinates from a squatted position over simmering pots. On the menu were snails, catla fish and emu egg fry.

"Mastanamma loved cooking for others, regularly feeding biryani to people and doling out pieces of spiced meat cooling on banana leaves to men working in the fields. She also loved her fans."

When Mastanamma died in 2018, aged 107, she was mourned by millions of devotees. Her funeral, like her, was suitably colourful. "To the thump of drums, a bright yellow truck carrying her body crawls along a dirt road," reported Suhasini Raj. "Well-wishers gather in the street, dancing, laughing, whistling and sprinkling the open coffin with hundreds of flower petals."

There's no need to feel daunted by this formidable role model. All of us grandmothers – from *cordon bleu* stars to sausage-and-chips queens – can take comfort instead from the food writer Anthony Bourdain's "Grandma Rule". "You may not like Grandma's Thanksgiving turkey," he explains in *Medium Raw*. "It may be overcooked and dry – and her stuffing salty and studded with rubbery pellets of giblet you find unpalatable in the extreme. You may not even like turkey at all. But it's *Grandma's* turkey. And you are in Grandma's *house.* So shut the fuck up and eat it."

My Grandmother's Dishes
by Lesléa Newman

are shaped like kidneys.
I don't know why
they have been boxed up

in my musty basement
for the past seven years
useless and forgotten

like my grandmother at the end
tucked away in the dreaded
nursing home. *God's waiting*

room, she called it, patting
my hand as if I were the one
in need of comfort.

"It takes a long time
to die, Mameleh," she said,
and she was right

it took her more than 99
years. But she is not gone
exactly. I inherited

her flat feet, her widow's
peak, her heart-shaped
locket complete

with a photo of my dashing
grandpa whom I never met
but was named for

and her kidney-shaped dish
set the color of Coney
Island's cold wet sand.

I dreamed of them last night
smooth and heavy in my hand
like they are this morning

when I set the table with them,
and suddenly I am sitting
in the one-tuchus kitchen

of my grandmother's fifth floor
walk-up. I can feel the yellow
vinyl seat of the chair

that always stuck to the back
of my thighs, I can hear
the honk and screech

of the Brooklyn traffic down
below, I can see my grandmother
in her rolled-down stockings

wearing her flowered apron
over her flowered housecoat,
her back to me as she stirs

something on the stove
that smells like the world
to come. But as she always

said, "Enough is enough."
It's time to give these dishes
to someone who could use them,

it's what she would want,
right? Wrong, says my dead mother
whose voice is never far

from my ear. If you don't
have to feed them and they aren't
hurting anybody, leave them

alone. Which is what she did
and which is why I have
the dishes that sat in her basement

for twenty-five years
now sitting in mine
which makes me wonder

where they will sit
after this daughterless
daughter is gone

Ten

Grannies on Film

Move over, femmes fatales, heartbreakers, wonderwomen and teenage rebels. It's time to make room for a new screen heroine: the grandmother. In the last 20 years or so, older women have joyfully invaded films and television shows, their characters reflecting how much the traditional views of grannies themselves have changed. Meet a host of unexpected, original, powerful and wise versions – and a few bad grannies.

"I like being old, young people are stupid," declares Ellie Reed, the 70-something star of the film *Grandma,* played by Lily Tomlin with irrepressible gusto. Ellie is an academic, a poet, a lesbian, who, intent on "transmogrifying her life", has cut up her credit cards and turned them into a wind chime. When her granddaughter Sage comes to her pregnant and in need of funds for an abortion, Ellie asks when her last period was. "Ten weeks ago," she whispers. "Mine was twenty-five years ago," announces Grandma.

First of all, she has to deal with Sage's appalling boyfriend who disappeared after discovering she was pregnant. So she punches him.

"Everyone's gonna talk about it at school!" frets Sage.

"What's he gonna say?" scoffs Grandma. "Sage's grandma beat me up?"

Then, in an attempt to raise the cash by collecting former debts, the pair set off on a road trip, visiting old haunts: coffee shops, tattoo parlours, former lovers.

Grandma celebrates an unconventional, outspoken, fearless feminist. The film critic Heather Hogan loved "her rage, her impetuousness, the exaggerated and reverent way she says 'Simone de Beauvoir'."

Other recent films present grannies who refuse to conform to the traditional stereotypes. *Bad Grandmas* features four seemingly unremarkable women whose quiet, conventional lives are upended when they accidentally kill a sleazy insurance agent. *Lucky Grandma* follows a Chinese American whose favourite pastimes are smoking and gambling. In Lee Isaac Chung's *Minari,* grandma Soon-ja is prone to swearing, wearing men's underwear and sneaking money from the church collection tray. In *The Proposal* Grandma Annie, played by Betty White, specialises in bad behaviour. She takes the grandchildren to see male strippers, and sees nothing wrong in faking heart attacks to get out of trouble.

And then there's *Book Club.* A group of older women – Sharon (Candice Bergen), Diane (Diane Keaton), Vivian (Jane Fonda) and Carol (Mary Steenburgen) – discover the joys of sex when they encounter *50 Shades of Grey.* Some are more enthusiastic than others. "If women our age were meant to have sex God wouldn't do what he does to our bodies," says Sharon. "To even be holding this book is embarrassing," agrees Carol. Vivian retorts, "I don't care what society says about women our age, sex must not be taken off the table."

Book Club may be a rather silly romp, but it's a glorious portrait of four good friends who are able to be frank about getting older – and to laugh about it.

Diane: "We're not eighteen anymore."

Carol: "No. We're sure not spring flowers."

Vivian: "No. More like potpourri."

The film was such a hit that *Book Club 2* arrived in 2023. This time the friends decide to take a trip to Europe, encountering predictable mishaps and adventures along the way. The sequel is even sillier than the original, but it carries the same spirit of resilience and hope. "Life is what you make of it," observes Sharon during one of their disasters. "So do something. Do something brave. Do something unexpected. But do something, because you have four women in a jail cell who are desperately hoping for a reason to believe there's still a reason to believe. So do something, goddammit, because this isn't the end of the freaking story."

And 2023 saw yet more daring grandmothers. *Maybe I Do* is a romcom featuring Diane Keaton and Susan Sarandon, and in *80 for Brady* those two heroines of liberation Jane Fonda and Lily Tomlin go on a road trip in a bid to spot their hero Tom Brady.

These rebellious screen heroines are proponents of what the critic Matt Brennan calls The Bad Grandma syndrome. "Unapologetic and at times unexpectedly crass, stylish, successful, and independent, the Bad Grandma resists the erasure of older women in American society by refusing to become invisible," Brennan explains. "The Bad Grandma, having cut her teeth in the women's rights movement of mid-century, recognises that feminism is a lifelong struggle, not a war that's been won. And she'll keep on fighting to the bitter end, ardently refusing to go quietly."

She's battling on the small screen, too. At the forefront of this new wave is *Grace and Frankie*, which, with seven series between 2015 and 2022, was Netflix's longest-running television show. Jane Fonda (Grace) and Lily Tomlin (Frankie) form an alliance when their husbands announce they are gay, in love and want to get married. It's a fight embraced with relish by the two actors. "I look at the positive side, the 'eff-you fifties', we call it," Fonda said. "Once you're over fifty it's like, who cares anymore?"

In one episode Grace screams at an unhelpful store clerk, distracted by flirting with a much younger customer, "Excuse me, are you in a coma? What kind of animal treats people like this?" Meanwhile Frankie steals a pack of cigarettes. "Can't see me, can't stop me," she says.

The series' own 'grandmother' is the earlier sitcom *The Golden Girls*, which aired from 1985 to 1992 with 180 half-hour episodes, and won a plethora of awards. It featured four older women living together in Miami, and was loved for its depiction of confident, sex-positive women over 50. It was also outspoken about social issues, including interracial dating, suicide, artificial insemination and even AIDS at a time when the disease was stigmatised. *The Golden Girls* may now seem tame, though, compared with the antics of *Grace and Frankie* – especially in how the latter deals with that most secret of pleasures: sex. In fact, it's obsessed with it and, in particular, the orgasm.

In Season 3 the two discuss the Menage a Moi, a Vybrand vibrator for geriatric women with arthritis. Fonda is shocked to be reminded how "big" they are. Tomlin replies that she'd never forgotten. Confronted with the real thing, she remembers thinking, "Well, jeez, these are so overstated, with these big old knobs on them and things like that." "Knobs are what matter," replies Grace. "God, we're gonna miss these gals." After that episode, when fans started to send her sex toys, she wasn't in the least bothered. "I'm a big fan of vibrators," Fonda admitted.

The Vybrand isn't the only strategy the two devise for living a more satisfying senior life. They praise the Riseup toilet, and Frankie swears by her yam lube.

Grace and Frankie may talk dirty, but they're always lovable. For a truly hateful bad granny, look no further than the foul-mouthed, cantankerous, impossible-to-please Nan, created by Catherine Tate for her BBC show.

In the early series of *The Catherine Tate Show* Nan's always in her armchair, being fairly civilised to visitors, but after they leave she criticises and rants about them. She complains to her grandson about her home help visitor, whom she refers to as a "fucking thief". She calls her new great-grandchild ugly. Her catchphrase, delivered at the crucial point of each sketch, is "What a fucking liberty!" In later series Nan spends less time in her armchair, which gives her the chance to be more offensive still. When she's in hospital she complains about her fellow patients, accuses a nurse of stealing from her and rejects the food menu: "I can't eat Chinese – their faces make me feel sick." In another sketch she's upset after attending the funeral of an old friend, until she realises that the deceased owed her £15. She's furious – especially as she'd spent another £25 on a wreath. In the 2005 Christmas special, Nan attends a Christmas party in an old people's care home. Charlotte Church makes a guest appearance as herself. When she starts to sing for the guests, Nan exclaims, "What a load of old shit!"

Nan goes even further afield in the 2022 film *The Nan Movie,* in which she travels to Ireland cross-country with her long-suffering grandson Jamie to visit her dying sister. Along the way she encounters a motley collection of characters – militant vegan arsonists, raucous rugby teams, crazed cops on motorbikes – providing yet more opportunities for her traditional mix of disapproval, fury and foul-mouthed put-downs.

But grandmothers don't have to be nasty to make it on to the screen. Three recent movies feature a quite different version of the granny: loving, powerful and wise.

Disney's 2016 animated film *Moana,* set on the Polynesian island of Motunui, sees grandmother Tala send the young Moana on a mission. Tala possesses the pounama stone, heart of Te Fiti, the goddess of nature. Now Moana must travel to the secret cave of ships to return it – and save the world. Tala prepares Moana for the journey by drawing on her fund of advice. "Sometimes our strengths lie beneath the surface… Far beneath, in some cases."

She adds her own recipe for every journey, for everyone. "It's called wayfinding, princess. It's not just sails and knots, it's seeing where you're going in your mind. Knowing where you are by knowing where you've been." Tala embodies the promise of all grandmothers. "There is nowhere you could go that I won't be with you."

In the Chinese film *The Farewell* an entire family, discovering that their beloved matriarch Nai-Nai has been given weeks to live, conspire to keep the news from her.

They even falsify the results of her medical tests to keep the diagnosis a secret from her, much to the horror of her granddaughter Billi. But Billi eventually agrees to join the cover-up when she realises that the deception is in keeping with the Chinese belief that a person's life is part of a whole, so it's the responsibility of the family to suffer on Nai-Nai's behalf.

She accepts, too, that when her grandmother gives her a *hóngbāo*, a gift of money in a traditional red envelope, she's also giving her a more lasting legacy. Billi doesn't want to accept the money, revealing that she's been rejected from the Guggenheim Fellowship she'd set her heart on. Nai-Nai encourages her to spend the money as she chooses. She needs to live her own life, she tells her, and not get hung up on this failure. "Don't be the bull endlessly ramming its horns into the corner of the room," she says. "Life is not about what things one does, but more so about how one goes about doing them."

Judi Dench, in *Belfast*, portrays a different kind of strength. When the family is planning to move to England, she decides to stay behind, but urges them to leave. "Go now – don't look back," she says at the end of the film. Those simple words evince a quiet selflessness that seems to encapsulate the courage, sacrifices and love that define what it is to be a grandmother.

Request to a Year
by Judith Wright

If the year is meditating a suitable gift,
I should like it to be the attitude
of my great- great- grandmother,
legendary devotee of the arts,

who having eight children
and little opportunity for painting pictures,
sat one day on a high rock
beside a river in Switzerland

and from a difficult distance viewed
her second son, balanced on a small ice flow,
drift down the current toward a waterfall
that struck rock bottom eighty feet below,

while her second daughter, impeded,
no doubt, by the petticoats of the day,
stretched out a last-hope alpenstock
(which luckily later caught him on his way).

Nothing, it was evident, could be done;
And with the artist's isolating eye
My great-great-grandmother hastily sketched the scene.
The sketch survives to prove the story by.

Year, if you have no Mother's day present planned,
Reach back and bring me the firmness of her hand.

Eleven

The Good, the Bad and the Terrifying

It's not just on screen that unexpected grandmothers are having their moment; they're beginning to make an appearance in literature, too. In Miriam Toews' 2022 novel *Fight Night* we meet the feisty, highly opinionated and pugnacious Elvira. She is the grandmother of nine-year-old Swiv, who is living in Toronto with her and with her mother. The novel is, as its title suggests, about fighting: the fight to survive, to find happiness and ultimately to live a good life. And at its heart is Swiv's exasperating, irrepressible Grandma Elvira.

When Swiv is expelled from school – for fighting – Grandma takes on the task of home-schooling, with her own brand of eccentric lessons: how to dig a winter grave, or write a letter using the words *one* and *blue*. For Maths: "If you've got a two-thousand piece puzzle of an Amish farm and you manage to add three pieces to the puzzle per day, how many more days will you need to stay alive to get it done?" The Amish puzzle refers to the family's Mennonite background, which often features in Toews' work. The women in *Fight Night* have had to fight the oppression they suffered in their village from the authoritarian leader and his male followers.

All Elvira's teachings, though, are really about how to fight. "Fighting can be making peace," she asserts. "Fighting can be going small."

Elvira is old and unwell, after endless health scares, but refuses to be defined by her frailty. When she has a fall in the kitchen she just laughs as Swiv helps her to her feet. After she drops her pills on the floor Swiv has to scramble around her feet picking them up – and also picking up hearing-aid batteries and conchigliette and pieces of the Amish farm puzzle.

She's prepared to travel to California to visit relatives, even though the long journey might, and eventually does, cause a heart attack. "To be alive means full body contact with the absurd," she maintains, adamant that she loves her body. "Still, we can be happy."

Sometimes hilarious, sometimes slapstick, *Fight Night* is also deeply serious. It's about defying despair, hardship and grief, and remembering, as Elvira puts it, that "we're here! We are all here now."

For irrepressible zaniness, meet Stephanie Plum's grandmother, in Janet Evanovich's series of crime capers. Stephanie is a not very successful bounty hunter who invariably ropes Grandma into her ill-fated quests to track down bail-avoiders. Grandma dresses young, spends her social security cheques on essentials like bowling shoes and occasionally watches pay-per-view porn, because "The Weather Channel doesn't have enough action."

Grandma Mazur goes to funerals for entertainment. She sometimes peeks underneath the casket lid to see the dead body. For one visit she sports chunky black heels and a lavender suit with a white blouse. Her bag is big enough to hold her .45 long-barrel which she carries at all times, unregistered of course, because she claims being old gives her a license to pack. Once, at the funeral parlour, she pulls it out and fires, inadvertently hitting one of the caskets and causing an explosion that burns down the funeral home. At Thanksgiving dinner one year she manages to shoot the turkey.

When preparing for a hot date, she gets Stephanie to shop with her. "I'm thinking I might have to show some skin," she explains. "I can open a couple buttons on my blue dress, but I can't get my boobs to stay up. I thought you might be able to get me one of them push-up bras." When she tries one, there's a problem. "I got them all lifted up, and they look pretty good except for the wrinkles."

Just as they're paying for the underwear, Stephanie is zapped with a stun gun by one of her rivals. Grandma couldn't be more delighted. Then, when she escorts Stephanie to her car, they find it has been spray-painted PIG CAR in black and white. "I would have used brighter colours," Grandma says. "Gold would have looked good! You can't go wrong with gold."

Children relish portrayals of naughty grandmothers. Foremost among them is David Walliams' wildly popular *Gangsta Granny*. She may seem like a dull, fussy old lady who smells of cabbage and likes playing Scrabble – but then her grandson Ben discovers that she's an international jewel thief. He persuades her to take him on a dangerous mission: to steal the crown jewels. And for sheer unrestrained nastiness there's Anthony Horowitz's *Granny*, who looks repulsive, smells of decomposing sheep and is out to destroy her hated grandson Joe.

None of the three protagonists in Sally Vickers' recent novel *The Grandmothers* is quite as wild as these creations, but each is unconventional in her own way. Nan has a special bond with nine-year-old Billy, whose parents are splitting up. Probably, she thinks, because his father is gay. Just like her own husband. Nan has a strict and somewhat idiosyncratic set of ethics. Principles, she explains, are really a cover for some form of power play, a roadmap for bullies. But she does value scruples, which she regards as a personal way to keep on the straight and narrow.

She rather disapproves of school. "'School teaches you to rely on what other people tell you. The trouble is they're either liable to tell you all wrong or stop you from finding out for yourself." Once, picking him up from school, she's summoned to his teacher. Billy, she's told, has been disciplined for swearing at another child, who had been teasing him for being "on the spectrum". She agrees to give him a serious telling-off, and on their way home offers him a deal.

"'You can have a quick slap and then come back to mine and no more said, or we can go back to yours and you can write a letter of apology to that girl.'

"'Smacking's illegal,' Billy said. 'You could go to prison.'

"'Ah, but who's to tell?' Nan asked. 'It'd be your word against mine.'"

After Billy opts for the smack she buys him a traffic-light lolly. "That's a reward for making up your own mind, not for the slap." She allows him to have sweets and cakes, in defiance of his mother's rules. "A little of what you fancy does you good," she explains.

Nan is also on a mission to teach her grandson how to lie. "It's not that I want you to deceive," she explains. "It's for self-protection... The important thing, Bill, is to know you're doing it Most people lie to themselves more than anything... And if you're going to lie the first rule is don't be found out."

Nan may seem like the traditional granny, adoring, loving, full of homespun wisdom and comfort food, but secretly she's a published poet, with a male pseudonym. Not even her publishers know her real identity, as she claims to be the poet's agent, and defends him from publicity.

Blanche is another fabricator of stories – but about her own life. Heartbroken when she is prevented from seeing her grandchildren, she is living a series of lies: drinking too much, shoplifting, inventing a secret lover. But she, too, has a real, hidden passion: for art. When she visits Paris, she is enchanted by a painting in the Louvre by Leonardo. It's a trinity – not the Trinity, but a different holy trio: St Anne, with her daughter Mary and her daughter's baby, Jesus. "St Anne, mother of the Virgin Mary, was sitting with her grown child on her lap, contemplating her daughter and the child her daughter in turn had borne. Mary, enlapped and enfolded by her mother, was oblivious to all but her baby boy, to whom she was reaching out in a beseeching gesture of love... Blanche observed how Mary's boy was looking back and up at his mother while her own mother, the boy's grandmother, gazed down at the two of them. And it seemed to Blanche that before her eyes the gazes of the three melted into a kind of moving reflection – mirroring and binding the three figures impalpably together in a never-ending play of encircling love."

To Blanche, and perhaps to Vickers too, that image is a perfect evocation of what it is to be a grandmother. "Quite clearly she could see in it the fond pride of a grandmother in her brand-new grandson. But she could see in the smile too – the thought like lightning struck her with an almost physical pain – the harrowing foreknowledge of all that lay ahead for this pair, in all the world closest to her heart, her dearest and most precious flesh and blood."

The third heroine, Minna, isn't really a grandmother. Something of a hermit, living in a caravan on the outskirts of Reading, she has developed a deep bond with Rosie through their shared fanciful imaginations. She, unlike Rosie's more literal parents, understands the girl's attachment to an army of toy animals who are given personalities and roles in endless fantasy games. The two were drawn together when Minna ran a book club at the school and Rosie was the only child who didn't walk out, bored with the choice of story. That story was *The Princess and the Gipsy* by George Macdonald, in which Princess Irene takes on and overcomes an army of evil goblins, with the help of a beautiful, mysterious lady, Irene's namesake and great-great-grandmother, who is suffused with magical powers.

It's unusual for a fairytale to give such a central role to a grandmother. In most tales grannies are frail and helpless, even when dispensing occasional wisdom. When older women do feature they tend to be evil stepmothers or wicked witches. The recent collection *Grandmothers' Stories: Wise Woman Tales from Many Cultures* aims to redress the balance, introducing us to older women who rescue children, weave magic, cast spells and outwit evil spirits. In the Swedish story "The Old Woman Who Was Right" a put-upon grandmother devises a sly plan to stem her cranky husband's endless carping. She suggests they swap roles for the day, to make him realise that running a farm is a piece of cake compared with housework and looking after the grandchild. Utterly defeated by the tasks he faces, he finally agrees never to complain again.

Fairy stories are also central in the Swedish novelist Fredrik Backman's captivating *My Grandmother Sends Her Regards and Apologises*. The story is told by Elsa, who is seven years old and "different". She's regarded as too sharp for her age, and she's constantly bullied at school. She reads a lot, loves Harry Potter and superhero comics, and is something of a pedant, always checking facts on Wikipedia and correcting misspelled signs with her red felt-tip pen.

Elsa's only friend is her eccentric, rule-defying grandmother, who cheats at Monopoly, drives in the bus lane, won't stand in line and steals IKEA carrier bags. When her smoking at the hospital sets off the fire alarm, "she starts ranting and raving about how 'everything *has to be* so bloody politically correct these days!'" And when two men knocked on the door wanting to talk about God and Jesus, "Granny stood on her balcony with her dressing gown flapping open shooting at them with her paintball gun."

But, Elsa tells us, Granny does tell the very best fairy tales ever. Every night she enchants Elsa with stories about far-off countries like the Land-of-Almost-Awake and the Kingdom of Miamas, where everybody is different and nobody needs to be normal. These places, Granny insists, "are not only real but actually far *more* real than the world we're in now, where 'everyone is an economist and drinks lactose-free milk and makes a right carry-on.'"

Granny's tales abound with princesses, dragons, knights and monsters – stories that are true or are, as she puts it, "other versions of the truth". When Granny dies, she leaves

Elsa instructions to deliver a series of letters apologising to people she has wronged. Although devastated at the loss of her grandmother, Elsa feels obliged to take on the mission. As she delivers the letters she begins to realise that her neighbours in the apartment building where she lives – a motley gathering of drunks, monsters, attack dogs, and old crones – are the real inhabitants of Granny's stories. Thus she discovers the connections between fairy tales and real life. Understanding truths about courage, love, loyalty and forgiveness will equip Elsa to deal with the loss of her superhero granny.

Death is also the theme of *The Summer Book*, by Finnish writer Tove Jansson, best known for her Moomin stories. In this lyrical evocation of love and loss we meet Sophie, whose mother has recently died and who is spending the summer on a beautiful, wild island which she explores with her lively, spirited grandmother. Over the course of the summer, Sophia and her grandmother explore the island's flora and fauna, spending hours in the "magic forest" and having long philosophical discussions. As Sophia's mother has died so recently, she often asks her grandmother about death and dying, and they speculate about what heaven might be like. When Sophia asks if angels can fly down to hell, her grandmother replies, "Of course. They might have all sorts of friends and neighbours down there." Her grandmother is quietly aware of the little girl's raw pain, so when Sophia is distraught over the loss of a palace they have made, she stays up all night to make a replacement. Gently, she helps Sophia to heal by showing her the beauty of the island, the power of nature.

Nor is she offended by Sophia's artless questions about her own mortality – "When are you going to die?" "Will they dig a hole?" Instead, she rather welcomes them. "She started thinking about all the euphemisms for death, all the anxious taboos that had always fascinated her. It was too bad you could never have an intelligent discussion on the subject. People were either too young or too old, or else they didn't have time."

As the story progresses it becomes clear that the old lady is approaching the end of her life. She has trouble with her balance and often loses her false teeth. But despite the book's melancholy mood there's a positive, happier theme too. The summer on the island has introduced Sophia to the pattern of the seasons, the cycle of life. Her grandmother, with her wise lessons, will live on in her.

Roald Dahl's most memorable grandmother, in *The Witches,* has her own way of introducing a child to the inevitability of death. She is, after all, not like most grandmothers. "My grandmother was the only grandmother I ever met who smoked cigars," remembers the boy narrator who comes to live with her after the death of his parents. "She lit one now, a long black cigar that smelt of burning rubber."

She is also, it transpires, an expert in the subject of witches – a Nazi-like international organisation of child-haters. With her grandson, she devises an elaborate plot to destroy them. But even she can't protect the little boy from their evil campaign to eliminate all children, and he is turned into a mouse. When the grandmother explains that mice, even human mice, don't really live for more than nine years, his reaction to his fate is an astonishing testament to the depth of his love.

"That's great!" he shouts. "It's the best news I've ever had!"

"Why do you say that?" she asks, surprised.

"Because I would never want to live longer than you. I couldn't stand being looked after by anybody else."

He then asks how old she is.

"I'm eighty-six," she says.

"Will you live another eight or nine years?"

"I might," she says. "With a bit of luck."

"You've got to. Because by then I'll be a very old mouse and you'll be a very old grandmother and soon after that we'll both die together."

"That would be perfect," she says.

Twelve

Rebels with Causes

Sisters are doing it for themselves, sang Aretha Franklin and Annie Lennox. Increasingly, that's what today's older women are doing too.

Take Iris Apfel, who until her death in 2024 had 2.9 million Instagram followers. Iris was known for her flamboyant outfits, oversized goggle glasses and refusal to give in to whatever is expected of older women. "I don't have any rules, because I'd only be breaking them," she announced.

Famous as a fashion influencer and style guru, she was celebrated in an exhibition at the Metropolitan Museum of Art, which said: "Her originality is typically revealed in her mixing of high and low fashions—Dior haute couture with flea market finds, 19th-century ecclesiastical vestments with Dolce & Gabbana lizard trousers."

Iris even had a Barbie doll based on her image. The doll wears a floral-patterned brocade suit with striped blouse, a plethora of necklaces and bracelets and, of course, her signature huge glasses, reflecting Iris's mantra, "More is more and less is a bore."

Iris said she never thought about her age. It was just a number. "Coco Chanel once said that what makes a woman look old is trying desperately to look young. Why should one be ashamed to be 84? Why do you have to say that you're 52? Nobody's going to believe you anyway, so why be such a fool? It's nice that you got to be so old. It's a blessing."

Here's how she introduced her book *Colourful: A Manifesto to Live a Bright, Bold Life.*

"This is not a book of secrets—I have no secrets. Sorry to disappoint if that's what you're looking for. I have some good stories, though. And a few ideas. This book is about living, creating, and colour. Because creativity and color matter. I don't want you to dress like me or think like me—that's not the idea of this book. I want you to find the colours, confidence, and creative inspiration that reflect you. My life has been filled with love, wonder, and a very deep, incurable curiosity. This book is my treasure trove of inspiration, influences, and ideas: My source. Be brave. Find your source. What makes you happy?"

Individual, fearless, rule-breaking women like Iris are part of a growing backlash against old-fashioned views of older women and, in particular, grandmothers. They are personified by Raging Grannies, a group of social activists who campaign across North America on peace and environmental causes, challenging stereotypical views of older women and the assumption that political action is only for the young.

In flamboyant outfits and with an irrepressible sense of fun as well as outrage, these are women over 50, some as old as 90, who are enraged by the conditions under which some people are forced to live, by threats to our environment, by war and by injustice wherever they find it.

During their 30 years of activism, Raging Grannies have held several anti-war rallies – and some went even further. In July 2005, five members of the group were charged with trespassing after they attempted to enlist at a US Army recruiting center in Tucson, Arizona. A spokesperson for the group said they wanted to be sent to Iraq so that their children and grandchildren could come home. A year later, another group, in New York City, were arrested for allegedly blocking access to a recruitment centre in Times Square. The Grannies have supported Black Lives Matter, and protested against genetically modified foods.

They represent so many grandmothers across the world who are no longer willing to remain invisible. A recent report by Age International, *Older Women: The Hidden Workforce*, highlights the enormous contribution these women make. It also reveals how much needs to change. According to Diane Elson, 75, an academic expert on gender and development as Emeritus Professor at the University of Essex, not only must women's work be recognised and valued, it must also be properly rewarded.

"I feel very passionate about the report," she told the charity. "I should, because it covers so many aspects of my own life, except that I'm so much more fortunate because I have a good pension. I'm a grandmother-carer, so tomorrow, I'll be collecting my granddaughter from school and looking after her, until her parents come home. It's something I enjoy, but it's a contribution, this unpaid care work that so many older women make in different ways around the world, which is very often invisible both to the policymakers and indeed often to their own families who take it for granted."

Age International's report demands proper acknowledgement of the economic contribution made by older women. But they are doing so much more, not just to help themselves but to help the world. Around the globe, groups of grandmothers have formed to campaign for political, social and economic change, and to work for peace, justice, education, health and human rights. In *Grandmother Power: A Global Phenomenon,* Paola Gianturco assembles an inspiring gallery of those determined to make a difference.

She meets grandmothers in India who are learning solar engineering and bringing light to their villages, and grandmothers in Argentina who have searched for more than a hundred grandchildren who were kidnapped during the military dictatorship, and have returned them to their families.

She is profoundly moved by the courage and resilience of African grandmothers. "While working in Kenya, Cameroon, Swaziland and South Africa, I met so many grandmothers raising AIDS orphans that it seemed to me the future of that continent rests with its grandmothers," she writes in her introduction. Over 14 million children who were orphaned by the disease were being cared for by their grandmothers.

Gianturco highlights the work of a unique cross-continent project, the *Grandmothers to Grandmothers Campaign,* whose members from Africa and Canada have got together to support and learn from each other. It was founded by the philanthropist Steve Lewis, who set up a charity to raise funds and create educational programmes to support them. In 2006 they published a joint statement defining their goals.

Acknowledging the struggles that they face, the African grandmothers stated: "We need training because the skills we learned while raising our children did not prepare us for parenting grandchildren who are bereaved, impoverished, confused and extremely vulnerable. We need security – regular incomes and economic independence... We grandmothers deserve hope."

The Canadian members added that they are committed to supporting their African partners, as "we are acutely conscious of the enormous debt owed to a generation of women who spent their youth freeing Africa, their middle age reviving it and their older lives sustaining it."

Meanwhile, Grandmothers in Switzerland have been engaged in a different kind of collective action. In April 2024 a group of older Swiss women won the first ever climate case victory in the European Court of Human Rights (ECHR).

The KlimaSeniorinnen, or Swiss Senior Women for Climate Protection, told the court that several of their rights were being violated. The group of 2500 women, known as the 'climate grannies', argued that because older women are more likely to die in heatwaves – which have become hotter and more common because of fossil fuels –Switzerland should do its share to stop the planet heating, and to abide by the Paris agreement target of 1.5C (2.7F) above preindustrial levels.

The court ruled that Swiss authorities had not acted in time to come up with a good enough strategy to cut emissions. It also found the applicants had not had appropriate access to justice in Switzerland.

According to the climate grannies the ruling demonstrated the power of older women and their refusal to be invisible. "They might be frail, some of them, in their body, but so fit in their head and so committed to something beyond themselves," said one of the Board members Elizabeth Stern. "We are not made to sit in a rocking chair and knit."

Many of the women have suffered from the effects of the heatwaves. But they are not just concerned for themselves. "This ruling is not just a victory for the Senior Women for Climate Protection. Our victory is a victory for all generations," commented Rosmarie Wydler-Walti, one of the group's leaders.

Joie Chowdhury, an attorney at the Centre for International Environmental Law campaign group, said the judgement would have a significant global impact. "We expect this ruling to influence climate action and climate litigation across Europe and far beyond."

The future of the planet also concerns another group of grandmothers, portrayed in Carol Schaefer's *Grandmothers Counsel the World: Women Elders Offer Their Vision for Our Planet.*

"We are deeply concerned with the unprecedented destruction of our Mother Earth, the atrocities of war, the global scourge of poverty, the prevailing culture of materialism, the epidemics that threaten the health of the Earth's peoples, and with the destruction of indigenous ways of life," declares the International Council of Thirteen Indigenous Grandmothers. "We believe that the teachings of our ancestors will light our way through an uncertain future…"

The Council's participants range from the Arctic to Brazil, Tibet to Mexico. All of them base their wisdom on faith and spiritual principles, and all practise the traditional medicines of their cultures. Among Mazatecs in Mexico, mushrooms are considered sacred. "Because we don't have money for doctors, we heal ourselves with mushrooms," says Grandmother Juliet, a healer whose patients include victims of AIDS, cancer, immune deficiency and stomach disorders. "The sacred mushrooms give you light. They give you the light of understanding, of knowledge, and the light of truth, wisdom and wonder."

Among Native Americans peyote is revered for its healing powers. Although it does cause hallucinations and delusions, Grandmother Margaret, from the Cheyenne nation, is adamant that it should never be used just to get high. In her practice she treats many alcoholics, and now sees it as her mission to free her people from alcohol and drug abuse and addiction.

"It has only been in the last 200 years that we have become chemically dependent," she says. "We can turn back to being the very powerful people we were... We need to be liberated from addiction and liberated from society's judgements. Even walking in the mountains is a high. Picking the wild turnips is a sacred practice. We have to remember that again."

Not everyone would put such faith in the power of natural healing to combat the world's ills. But what is compelling is these women's conviction that the wisdom of the past must be retained and reinforced. "There is no way to replace intergenerational knowledge of how to live sustainably, how to reaffirm relationship," Schaefer writes in her introduction.

That view is echoed by the campaigning feminist Gloria Steinem, who sees a connection between her own suffragette grandmother and the values of the Grandmothers Council. "I have faith that, if we do the hard work of learning what has gone before us," she tells Schaefer, "taking on the pain of others, as well as their pleasures, of honoring the self-authority of each person, including ourselves, then these days will have made us a multitude."

This commitment to preserving the environment and to resisting the encroachment of destructive technologies is shared by many grandmothers in the UK as well. A study by the Centre for the Understanding of Sustainable Prosperity found that Extinction Rebellion has "a much broader and more diverse age profile than has been the case for the previously small networks of mainly young activists". These older protestors mean business.

"The newspapers have been full of pensioners who have been getting themselves arrested: the Welsh 82-year-old, the Oxford 81-year-old and, perhaps most impressively, the 91-year-old from Kent," writes Ben Sixsmith in his Unherd essay "How Grannies Became the New Frontline Activists". He suggests that "maybe older activists feel more responsible for environmental decay, with one nonagenarian telling *Sky* that it was 'his generation that had caused the damage that led to climate change.' Perhaps, too, having already enjoyed a long life and career, they find it easier to imagine living out the rest of their time on Earth in a more restrained fashion."

Putting old people on the frontlines of environmental activism also makes tactical sense, Sixsmith says, citing Polly Toynbee, who, two years ago, wrote a column called "How Older People Became the Heroes of Extinction Rebellion". She claimed that they are the best "'arrestables' ... free of children, with pensions. They have no need to worry about damaged CVs and criminal-record checks, and so are model protest material, with the least to lose. Police, mainly easy on arrestees of all ages, are doubly wary of dragging older folks down the street.

"There is some history here: Bertrand Russell being arrested at the age of 89 at a protest against nuclear weapons gained recognition on both sides of the pond, as well as Walter Wolfgang's forcible ejection from the 2005 Labour Party conference at the age of 82, after he had shouted 'nonsense' at Jack Straw for defending the invasion of Iraq. The rough treatment of old people, rightly or wrongly, inclines us to feeling more sympathetic towards the geriatric rabble-rousers. This same sympathy is rarely extended upon the rough treatment of the young... Putting kindly old people in front of the cops is smart. If you happen to be organising your own protest you could take a worse lesson."

Whether you're planning to mount the barricades, shout out on Instagram, organise food boycotts or just flaunt your ageing style, you and all grandmothers have a shared goal: to do what you can to make the world better for the next generation. The best way to achieve that is to fill those children with love, strong values, goodness and a commitment to an ethical life.

This book is printed on paper from sustainable sources managed under the Forest Stewardship Council (FSC) scheme.

It has been printed in the UK to reduce transportation miles and their impact upon the environment.

For every new title that Troubador publishes, we plant a tree to offset CO_2, partnering with the More Trees scheme.

MORE TREES
LET'S PLANT A BILLION TREES

For more about how Troubador offsets its environmental impact, see www.troubador.co.uk/sustainability-and-community